Cataloging-in-Publication Data

—

kers : official American Mensa game book / Robert

ecker problems.   I. American Mensa Limited.

9

98–48172
CIP

Edited by Peter Gordon

4   6   8   10   9   7   5   3

ISBN 1-4392-4385-9

P
C

Library of Congres
Pike, Robert W., 19.
Play winning che
Pike
p.   cm.
Includes index.

1. Checkers. 2. C
II. Title
GV1463.P58   199
793.2—dc21

Contents

Preface
7

A Checkers Perspective
9

Part One: Checker Terms and Fundamentals
11

Computerized Checkers and Chinook
31

Part Two: Strategy and Tactical Considerations
33

The Greatest Checker Player Ever: Dr. Marion Tinsley
93

Checker Tournaments
94

Tournament Scorecard
96

Answers
98

The Other Classic Positions and How to Play Them
103

The Longest Stroke Problem and Solution
109

Rules of Play and Laws for Standard American Checkers
111

Variations of the American Standard Game
115

Index
124

Preface

Checkers is a universally popular game for all ages that has provided countless hours of enjoyment for all of its players, from youthful beginner to dedicated grandmaster. There is plenty of interaction involved with every checker contest, so in addition to the pleasure factor, this great game also builds important social skills. The mental challenges created by the dynamic series of ongoing problem-solving situations do a great deal to develop players' thinking skills, including:

- Analyzing alternative solutions
- Improving attention span and concentration
- Encouraging perseverance
- Considering different strategies
- Recognizing geometric patterns
- Dealing patiently with complex situations

All of the above have a positive effect on students from an educational standpoint. These same attributes can also be of significant value in many everyday activities.

With the proliferation of computer technology (and checkers is no exception to the onslaught of machine games, which will be discussed later in this book), checkers is one of the very few multigenerational, interactive games left that everyone knows and likes to play. There is a rarely found common ground for everybody with checkers. It is not age related and requires no special physical ability. Nor is it contingent on social, economic, or political status. It is truly inclusive.

Many checker players, including this author, have fond memories of learning the game from their parents or grandparents in a social setting that taught them the invaluable traits of sportsmanship and how to win and lose graciously.

We hope this book will improve your checker-playing performance while enhancing the enjoyment you derive from the simplistic elegance and astonishing maneuvers involved with what has proven to be, for more than 50 centuries, one of the most thought-provoking games the world has ever known.

Throughout this book, masculine pronouns are used. This is done for simplicity, and should not be taken to mean that only males can play checkers. And now, as we say in checker parlance, "it's your move."

Think ahead.

—Robert Pike

A Checkers Perspective

Although almost everyone has played checkers, which is enjoyed all over the world, nobody knows exactly how old it is or even where this "granddaddy of boardgames" started. The discovery of hieroglyphic drawings on King Tut's pyramid in Egypt depicting two checker players matching wits on an identifiable checkerboard has been archeologically traced back to around 3000 B.C., making the game at least 5000 years old! But it might easily predate that calculation by millenniums and may very well have originated elsewhere.

This probably makes checkers the oldest boardgame in the world. It's older than chess, older than dominoes, and even older than Chinese checkers. It must be a wonderful game to have lasted this long and still be going strong today.

Checkers has many different names in various parts of the world, such as "draughts" (pronounced "drafts") in England and "juego de damas" or "fechas" in Hispanic countries. But no matter what name it's known by, people around the globe recognize the familiar checkerboard pattern.

The captivating charm of the game is directly related to its elegantly simplistic rules that even a youngster can easily understand, combined with beautifully conceived combinations of movement, great depth of strategic thought, and surprising tactics that make checkers extremely difficult, if not impossible, to master.

Because their playing boards are identical, checkers and chess have often been compared with each other. Checkers almost always suffers in these comparisons by many who elevate chess, because of its much more convoluted rules structure, onto a pedestal of greater intellectual superiority. In fact, both checkers and chess have countless numbers of intricate, mind-boggling plays.

Edgar Allan Poe weighed in on the side of checkers when he wrote in his *Murders in the Rue Morgue* that "I hereby take occasion to assert that the higher powers of the human intellect are more decidedly and more usefully tasked by the unostentatious game of Draughts, than by all the elaborate frivolity of Chess. In the latter, where the pieces have different and bizarre motions, with various and variable values, what is only complex is mistaken (a not unusual error) for what is profound."

Over the years, the game and the rules have evolved to the point where a large majority of checker players follow the dictates of the American Checker Federation (ACF) and the British Draughts Federation (BDF), which are practically identical. These rules, found on page 111, are used throughout this book. There are numerous checker game variations, many of which are discussed in the section that begins on page 115.

And now, in the age of computerization, with the analysis and playing of games being one of the computer's great attributes, checkers is enjoying another rejuvenation. In 1994, the dedicated checker-playing computer Chinook, which was programmed, developed, and fine-tuned by Dr. Jonathan Schaeffer et al. at the University of Alberta, Canada, won the World Man vs. Machine Championship* in a defaulted match with the late Marion Tinsley— indisputably the greatest human checker player in the history of the game. These subjects are covered in greater length later in this book.

No individual or computer has since been able to win a match against Chinook, which readers can play against (up to advanced skill levels) on the Web at http://www.cs.ualberta.ca/~chinook. It is doubtful that any individual human will be able to beat Chinook playing at full strength under the present rules. Another exceptionally powerful computer application, developed by Gil Dodgen and Ed Trice of World Championship Checkers (InfinteLS on the Internet), could very well prove to be a serious challenger for the Canadian king's crown in a machine vs. machine contest.

Tinsley described the experience of competing with this omnipotent, chip-driven automaton to that of a world-class weightlifter being pitted against a fork-lift truck that has no human frailties and never gets tired.

Only time will tell what long range effects computers will have on this grand old game. They have already become more than worthy opponents for the checker aficionado without a partner who wants to play against an estimable competitor. Meanwhile, checkers will continue to captivate many of those who delve in to try to solve its fascinating mysteries. Machine vs. machine, human vs. machine, rule changes, and checker-power alterations (such as 11 men per side) all offer exciting developmental possibilities. And no one knows what else will happen on the mystical squares to keep this marvelous game vigorously alive and well for at least another 5000 years!

One Jump Ahead by Jonathan Schaeffer (Springer-Verlag New York, 1997) tells this interesting story in detail.

PART ONE

Checker Terms and Fundamentals

The Equipment

The name "checkers" is derived from the disklike pieces used in play. The game is played on a square checkerboard made up of 64 smaller squares. Thirty-two of these squares are light colored and alternate on the board from row to row and column to column with the 32 darker squares as shown below in Diagram 1.

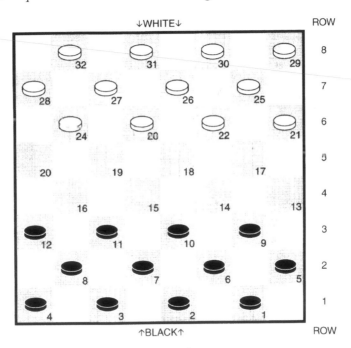

Diagram 1

A numbered gray-and-white checkerboard properly aligned with the black and white checkers on their appropriate starting squares.

Checkerboard Patterns and Numbering

The gray squares are the only ones that are played on in the game. The checkerboard is always made up of two different colors, and the darker of the two are the ones to use for the match. The check-

11

ers never move onto or over the white or lighter colored squares in any direction. These squares are only there to form the checkerboard pattern. While it is not absolutely necessary, it is very helpful to have each of the dark squares numbered from 1 to 32 as shown above in Diagram 1. These numbers make it much easier to follow the moves that are described in this or any checker publication. This also facilitates the annotation or recording process that many serious checker players undertake in order to be able to review and analyze their games. Without this, or some other system that identified the dark squares, it would be very difficult to keep track of all the moves. Although annotation is rarely done during informal games, it is standard procedure during championship-level tournament matches. The following is an example of an annotated series of moves by two contestants (the darker checkers always go first):

	Black	White
1.	11–15	23–19
2.	8–11	22–18
3.	15–22	25–18
	(jump)	(jump)
4.	11–16	24–20

You can follow these moves on the fold-out checkerboard that's tucked inside the back cover. Use pennies and dimes for black and white checkers.

Positioning the Board
The checkerboard should be positioned so that one of the two light-colored squares (unnumbered and not to be played on) is on each player's right-hand side. "Light on the right" is a good way to remember this when playing on an unnumbered board. (You can easily number an unnumbered board using the sequence shown in Diagram 1.) With numbered boards, it is virtually impossible to position the board and checkers incorrectly because of the numbers running horizontally across the board from row to row, which almost force the board into the proper alignment.

Checker Placement to Start the Game
Before the game starts, the 12 black checkers are placed on each of the 12 gray squares numbered 1 to 12 in the first three rows (rows 1, 2, and 3), and the twelve white checkers are positioned on each of the gray squares in rows 6, 7, and 8 on the opposite end of the board that are numbered 21 to 32. This is shown in Diagram 1.

Deciding Who Goes First

The player with the darker checkers always goes first. The decision as to who will have the darker checkers can be decided by the flip of a coin or by selecting one of the opponent's two closed fists that conceal a dark checker in one hand and a light checker in the other. The player who has the darker checkers in the first game gets the lighter checkers in the second game. Players continue to alternate this way, game after game.

Some players like to go first because they think it's an advantage to be a move ahead. Other players prefer to go second, figuring that they can move to a more strategically advantageous position after seeing the opponent's first move. Years of play and analysis have proven that players have an exactly equal opportunity in the game whether they go first or second—there is no advantage.

Color Considerations

Any combination of light and dark colors can be used for the checkerboard and checkers. Red and black checkers moving on the black squares of a red and black checkerboard are the traditional standards. But the American Checker Federation officially specifies a board made up of green and white squares with red and white checkers moving on the numbered green squares. These "Christmas colors" are more visually appealing and do a better job of distinguishing the checker pieces from their squares—black checkers on black squares are hard to see.

Opening Moves

With the board and checkers positioned properly, the player with the black checkers moves one of the four checkers in his front row (from squares 9, 10, 11, or 12 in row 3) diagonally forward to one of the empty adjacent gray squares in the row immediately ahead (row 4). Then it's white's turn, and white can move any one of the four checkers in his front row (from squares 21, 22, 23, or 24 in row 6) diagonally forward to one of the empty adjacent gray squares in the row ahead (row 5). The arrows in Diagram 2 show the seven different first moves that are available to black and the seven that white can make on his subsequent opening move.

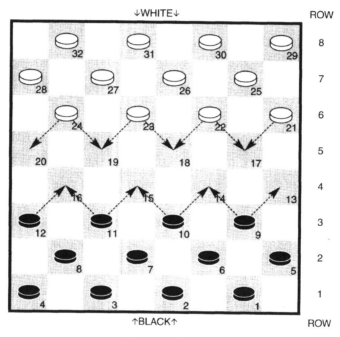

Diagram 2

The arrows show the seven different moves that black can make to start the game and the seven choices white has in responding to black's opening move.

Single Checker Movements

Throughout the game the single checker pieces ("checkers" or "men") can only move diagonally forward, one square per move, to an adjacent empty gray square in the row immediately ahead. The black checkers must move from their 12 starting squares in rows 3, 2, and 1 forward toward row 8. The white checkers must move in the same manner from their initial locations on the 12 squares in rows 6, 7, and 8 toward row 1. Players take alternating turns. First black goes, then white, then black again, and the players continue to alternate turns this way throughout the game.

Jumping and Capturing
When it's a player's turn to go and there is an opponent's checker on either of the diagonally adjacent gray squares in the row directly ahead with an empty gray square on the same diagonal line in the following row, he *must* jump over the opponent's checker and land on the aforementioned empty gray square. This action constitutes capturing the jumped-over checker. The player making the capturing jump removes the captured checker from the board and places it in a holding area off to the side where it can later be used to crown an opponent's king (discussed on pages 20–21) or to start a new game after the one being played is completed. This compulsory jumping rule is very important to the game of checkers and how it's played, so it's illustrated below in Diagram 3 for clarity.

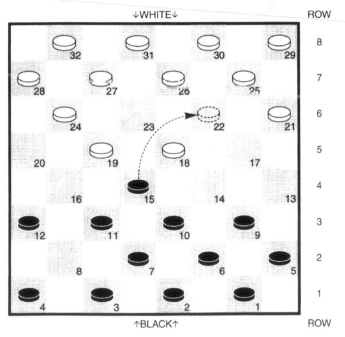

Diagram 3
A jumping opportunity for black from the annotated moves/jumps listed on page 12. White's second move from 22 to 18 gave the black checker on 15 the chance to jump from 15 to 22. Black must take this jump and remove the white checker on 18 from the board.

Double Jumps

If, after a player makes a capturing jump to an empty square, there is another one of the opponent's checker pieces on either of the two diagonally adjacent gray squares in the next row ahead with an empty gray square on a diagonal line in the following row, the jumping player *must* continue on with another jumping/capturing leap to that empty gray square. This is shown in Diagram 4.

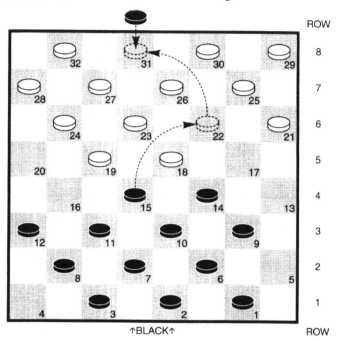

Diagram 4

A double jump for black. In this situation, after the black checker on 15 has jumped to 22, there is another jumping opportunity for that black checker to jump over the white checker on 26 to the empty square numbered 31. Black must also take this jump and remove the white checkers on squares 18 and 26 from the board. Since square 31 is in the king row, black's checker gets crowned to become a king.

Triple Jumps

After a double jump, if there is still another one of the opponent's checker pieces on either of the two diagonally adjacent gray squares in the next row ahead with an empty gray square on a diagonal line in the row after that, then the player who made the double jump would have to take a third capturing jump over the opponent's checker piece and land on the empty gray square for a triple jump! This is illustrated below in Diagram 5.

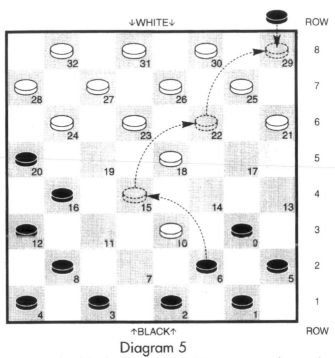

Diagram 5

A triple jump. The black checker on 6 jumps over three white checkers going from 6 to 15 to 22 to 29 in the king row, where the opponent places another black checker on top of it to make it a king.

A single checker never gets more than a triple jump because if it lands in the king row (row 8 for black and row 1 for white) on the third leap of a triple jump, it has to stop and be crowned a king by having one of the same-colored checkers from the opponent's holding area placed on top of it. This crowning action (usually done by the opponent as a courtesy) is the end of the newly crowned king's turn. Diagram 5 shows this.

If the player with the triple jump started from his back row (row 1 for black and row 8 for white), the checker making the triple jump would land on a gray square in the next-to-last row (row 7 for black and row 2 for white), where there are no more forward-jumping opportunities. This situation is depicted in Diagram 6.

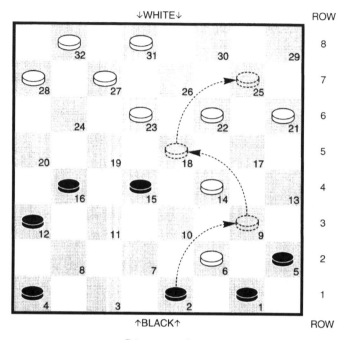

↓WHITE↓   ROW

↑BLACK↑   ROW

Diagram 6

Black makes a triple jump from 2 to 9 to 18 to 25 in row 7, where there are no more forward jumping possibilities for this single checker.

Choosing Between Jumps When There's More Than One

If a player has two or more jumping opportunities when it's his turn to go, he may select any one he wants to take, even it is inferior in regard to the number and/or type of pieces captured or in the position it ends up in. Diagram 7 shows three jumping opportunities for black. While jump B is obviously the best, because it is a double jump to the king row, black could choose either A or C instead of B, even though both of these alternatives would prove to be a serious error in judgment. If black took Jump A, from 16 to 23, white would double-jump from 18 to 11 to 2 for a king and a nine-to-eight checker-power lead with black in all sorts of jeopardy. Should black select jump C, white would triple-jump back from 27 to 18 to 11 to 2 for a king and an almost certain victory.

18

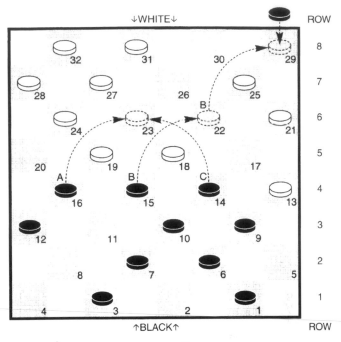

↑BLACK↑ ROW

Diagram 7

Black has three jumping opportunities here (A, B, and C). Jump A is from 16 to 23. B is from 15 to 22 to 29. C is from 14 to 23. Although jump B is much better than A or C, black can take whichever one of the three jumps he wants to.

The Rationale for Compulsory Jumping

The compulsory jumping rule was introduced in the late 19th century. It has done a great deal to improve the play of the game and has made it more exciting. Prior to this rule (that you must jump when you have the opportunity), if a player had a jump and didn't take it, the opponent could a) point it out and require him to retract the move and make the jump(s), b) let the move stand and remove the checker that didn't jump from the board just as if it had been captured and then make his own move, or c) let the move stand and then make his own move. But the severity of these penalty options (called the "huffing rule") seemed to be unfair in relation to such a relatively innocent oversight, so the rule was changed and simplified to make jumps compulsory. Under the current rules, if players refuse to jump after being advised of the opportunity, they lose the game by forfeit—so it doesn't make any sense to refuse to jump.

19

The Importance of Kings and How to Get Them

One of the best ways to improve the chances of winning a game of checkers, or at least drawing, is to promote single checker pieces to king status by moving and/or jumping all the way up the board with them and onto one of the four gray squares in their king row on the opposite end of the playing field (row 8 for black and row 1 for white) as shown in Diagram 8.

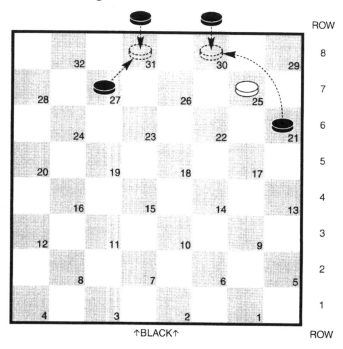

Diagram 8

Black gets a king by moving into the king row from 27 to 31 and by jumping into the king row from 21 to 30. In both cases the opponent crowns the black checker by placing another black checker on top of it. This designates it as a king and ends the turn.

Crowning the King

When a player moves or jumps into the king row with a checker, the opponent designates it as a king by crowning it, which consists of placing another checker of the same color on top of it. This crowning action also ends the newly crowned player's turn. Now it becomes the opponent's turn to go. This is illustrated in Diagram 9 with both a move and a jump into the king row by black.

20

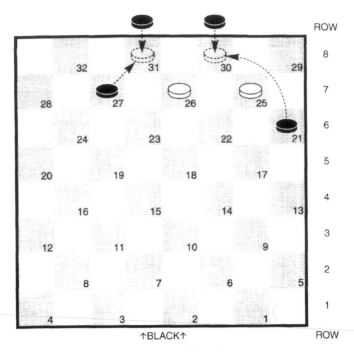

↑BLACK↑   ROW

Diagram 9

The crowning action that is done when a single checker reaches the king row ends that player's turn. Black's newly crowned
kings cannot jump and capture the white checker on 26
because black's turn has ended. White, whose turn it is, would
in most situations move this checker to 22 or 23 to avoid being
jumped.

While this termination-of-the-turn rule enables the other player to
move a threatened piece away from the immediate danger of being
jumped, in certain circumstances it also provides the opponent with
an opportunity to set up a multiple-jumping sequence of his own by
not moving a piece that is in jeopardy of being captured by the
newly crowned king and, instead, using his move to position another one of his pieces so as to take devastating advantage of the new
monarch's forced jump. This Machiavellian tactic is shown in
Diagrams 22, 47, 48, and 62.

How the Kings Move and Jump

Kings are much more powerful than regular checkers because they can move and jump diagonally backward as well as forward on the gray squares. This ability to move and jump in both directions makes the kings extremely flexible and dangerous to the opponent, as seen in Diagram 10.

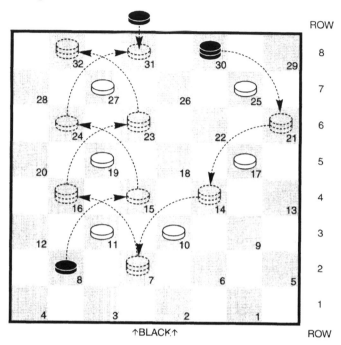

Diagram 10

The black king on 30 jumps all six of white's checkers by going from 30 to 21 to 14 to 7 to 16 to 23 to 32. The black checker on 8 can capture only three white pieces, by jumping from 8 to 15 to 24 to 31.

Demonstrating the King's Jumping Prowess

Kings have such extensive maneuverability that they could jump as many as nine of the opponent's pieces in one series of ongoing leaps, if the opponent's checkers were placed as shown in Diagram 11. While this would probably never happen in a real game, because no one would be so foolish as to position his checkers this way, it does demonstrate the awesome power of a king! This intimidating strength encourages players to try to get kings as early as possible in order to greatly improve their chances of capturing the other player's pieces to win the game.

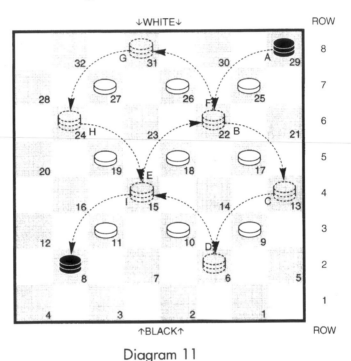

Diagram 11

The black king on 29 jumps to 22 to 13 to 6 to 15 to 22 to 31 to 24 to 15, and finally to 8, taking all nine of white's pieces off the board.

Winning—The Usual Way

There are three ways to win a game. The most common method is to capture all of the opponent's checkers. Diagram 12 shows black winning the game with a triple jump that captures all of white's remaining pieces.

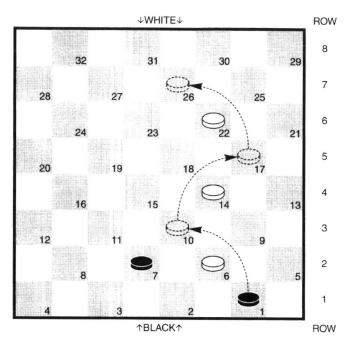

Diagram 12

The black checker on square 1 gets a triple jump that removes all of white's remaining pieces from the board and wins the game.

Blocking the Opponent to Win

Another, much less frequently occurring victory can be secured by blocking all of the opponent's pieces so he cannot move or jump anywhere when it's his turn to go. If a player cannot move when it's his turn, he loses the game, even if the player who is unable to move has more pieces on the board. This is illustrated in Diagram 13 below. While blocking opportunities do not come up very often, alert players can make them happen in certain circumstances and, conversely, they are careful not to place their checkers in a position where an opponent can lure them into a blocked position. Although white has just one king left on the board, it's blocking all three of the black pieces so they cannot move or jump anywhere. So, white wins.

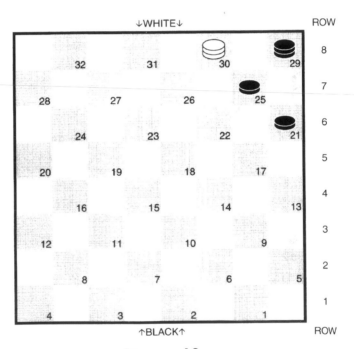

Diagram 13

Black has a king and two checkers blocked in a single corner by white's king on 30. It's black's turn to go, but none of the black pieces can move or jump anywhere (a king can't jump its own checker), so black loses because he can't move when it's his turn to go, even though he outnumbers white three to one.

Forfeit or Surrender

The third means of winning is when the opponent gives up. This may happen if a player becomes hopelessly behind in checker power or he determines that he is in a position where he is certain to lose in a few more moves. Diagrams 14 and 15 below show these two types of situations, where it would be more prudent to surrender, rather than waste time by continuing to play with an inevitable defeat in plain sight. But it is very important to try to find a way to overcome a manpower deficit or a difficult position with moves that could tie, or even win, instead of giving up too easily, because sometimes you might be able to do so, as illustrated in Diagram 16.

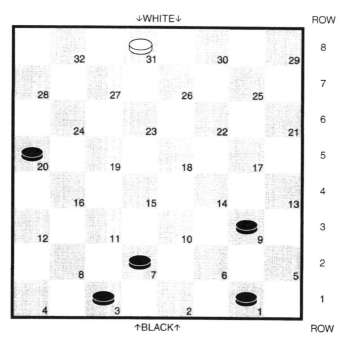

Diagram 14

White surrenders here because black outnumbers him five to one and there is no realistic way for white to overcome such a huge checker-power deficit.

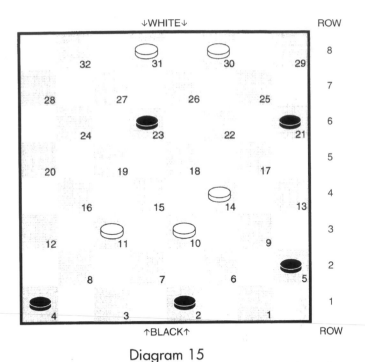

Diagram 15

It's black's move and he is in an impossible positional predica-
ment from which there is no escape. Every move black makes
will give white an unanswered jump, so black resigns.

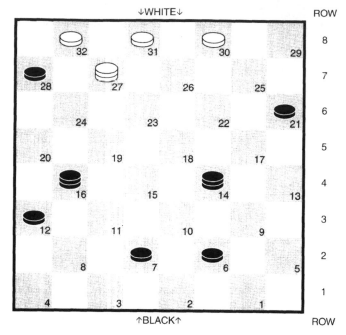

↑BLACK↑

Diagram 16

White prevails in what looks like a lost game. First white sacrifices by moving from 30 to 25. Black has to jump from 21 to 30 and gets another king. Then white sacrifices again, going from 31 to 26, and the new black king must jump from 30 to 23. This gives white's king on 27 a game-winning quintuple jump to 18 to 9 to 2 to 11 to 20. Black can only move his checker on 12 to 16 and be jumped.

Frequently Asked Questions

Beginners often ask the following questions:
- Can a single checker jump and capture a king? Yes, it must, and it takes the entire king off the board, not just the crown.
- Can a king jump over its own checker or another one of its own kings? No, it cannot.
- Can a player split up a king to make two single checker pieces? No, he cannot.
- Does a king get any additional powers if it returns to the opponent's king row on the other end of the board? No, it does not.
- Can a king jump and capture an opponent's king? Yes, it must!
- What do you do if there are no checkers in your holding area to crown an opponent's king? Place one of the other colored checkers underneath it or a coin on top of it to identify it as a king.
- What happens if you have a jump, but you don't see it? Your

28

opponent has to point it out and you have to take it.

- What happens if there is a jump to be taken and neither player sees it? Play would continue until the jump is seen and it is then taken in turn.

Ties or Draws

Although many checker games are won by one of the previously described methods, sometimes both players agree to declare the game a tie or a draw when neither can find a way to win. This happens quite often, especially in games between expert players who make very few mistakes. One of the most common draws occurs when both players have one king apiece or two kings each and are chasing one another around in one of the two double corners (the corner squares on each player's right-hand side that are numbered 1 and 5 for black and 28 and 32 for white). Unless one player makes a careless move, neither will be able to force a win, so they agree to call it a draw since there is no sense in moving around indefinitely in the double corners. This kind of situation is shown in Diagram 17.

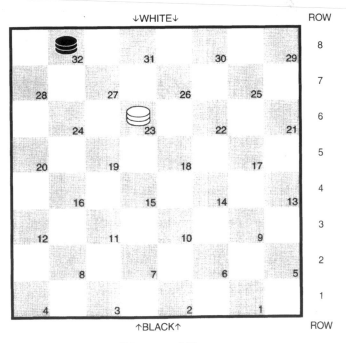

Diagram 17

It's black's move and it is a double corner standoff. In this situation, neither player can force a win. They will move around in the double corner area indefinitely, unless one player makes a careless mistake, so they usually agree to call it a tie game.

Offering a Draw and Refusing an Offer of a Draw

If a player thinks the game is going to result in a tie, he can offer the opponent the option of declaring the game a draw. The opponent then has two choices. He can accept the draw or refuse it. If he accepts, the game stops and is declared a draw. If, however, the opponent thinks that he is in a position to win and refuses to accept the draw offer, then that player must find a way to win the game in 40 moves or fewer for each side. If the refusing player cannot achieve victory within this 40-move-per-side limit, the game is declared a draw (unless the player who had offered the draw discovers a previously unforeseen way to win during the 40-move-per-player limitation period).

Official Rules

The official rules of the American Checker Federation are listed on page 111 with suggestions for some less stringent interpretations for informal, non-tournament games to create a more easygoing atmosphere, because we should always remember that checkers is a game to be enjoyed. So the most important rule of all is to have fun—win, lose, or draw!

Computerized Checkers and Chinook

The simplicity of the rules, the small number of pieces involved (checkers and kings), and their limited movements (moves and jumps), stimulated early efforts to use the artificial intelligence of computers to master the game of checkers. The first checker computer systems were developed by programmers who were naively unaware of the depth of thought required to play successfully at the higher levels of expertise. Consequently, their machines fared well against the rank and file players, but failed miserably in face-to-screen confrontations with the grandmasters.

In 1989, Dr. Jonathan Schaeffer (pictured), professor of computer science at the University of Alberta, Canada, put together a team (including a checker expert) to begin work on a program that would solve this mysterious game and defeat the world champion (Marion Tinsley or whoever it might be). Schaeffer, a master chess player, had already developed a world-class computerized chess program, so the challenge appeared to be relatively easy. It was not! He and his formidable group fine-tuned their electronic prodigy, which they named Chinook, over a five-year period, to the point where it was recognized as the world champion of checkers in 1994. Although Chinook never actually defeated Tinsley outright in a match, it did wrest this title from him, during what was to be a 40-game contest, when Tinsley had to resign and defaulted (with the match standing even at seven draws) due to a sudden illness that took his life the following year.

Interestingly, IBM's "Deep Blue" chess computer bested Garry Kasparov, the "unbeatable" world chess champion, three years later.

It is doubtful if human players will be able to defeat the upgraded version of Chinook and its lookalike automatons. If perchance they should, the programmers will simply do some more educated tweaking to move their robotic marvels even closer to the status of perfection that they have already come so close to achieving.

Schaeffer's book, *One Jump Ahead* (Springer-Verlag New York, 1997), tells the intriguing story of Chinook in a way that will fascinate both checker players and computer devotees.

Interested players can match wits against Chinook on the World Wide Web at http://www.cs.ualberta.ca/~chinook (it's free). There are numerous other challenging checker games available on the Web and in software form, including World Championship Checkers, which was mentioned earlier, via an Internet search.

PART TWO

Strategy and Tactical Considerations

Checkers is one of the few games in the world where luck never plays a part, unless you consider your opponent's bad moves as good luck for you or that your mistakes are unlucky. Most card and dice games have lots of strategic possibilities that skillful players utilize in their efforts to win, but Lady Luck can also play an important part in those contests with the receipt of good or bad cards or by rolling out favorable or unfavorable numbers on the fickle cubes. Even in athletic sports, fortune can smile or frown on the participants when their ball hits the goal post and caroms in or out. The related saying "That's the way the old ball bounces" is one with which everybody identifies. But checker games are won by the player who makes the most skillful moves and/or the fewest mistakes. If both players play equally well, a checker game is likely to end up in a tie. And numerous games between master checker players result in a draw because both contestants play so well game after game. Consequently, strategic thinking and carefully planned tactical moves are all the more important in checkers, since there is no way that good luck can rescue a player who has gotten himself into a difficult situation, and no one can logically use bad luck as a valid excuse for losing a game as a result of his judgmental errors.

The following text, with its supportive diagrams, is aimed at developing an insightful understanding of the strategy and tactics that will improve a player's game as well as the enjoyment he derives from it. In all of the following discussions it would be extremely helpful to use a numbered checkerboard and checkers to set up the positions and actually make the moves and jumps that are described. This exercise will greatly enhance clarity and understanding.

A game of checkers can be divided into three overlapping phases. It starts with the opening and early game when both players are at, or close to, full strength. They jockey for position during the first eight or nine moves as shown in Diagram 18.

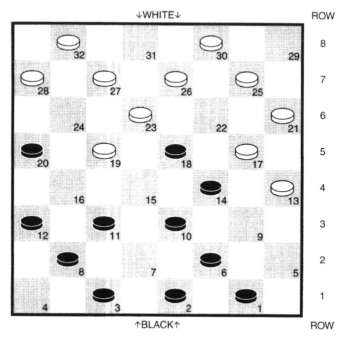

Diagram 18

An early game situation with both players at equal strength. It's black's move and he finds a beautiful way to forge ahead. Can you find the way? (Answers to problems begin on page 98.)

Next comes the middle game, after several jumping/capturing exchanges have taken place during the subsequent series of moves. Diagram 19 depicts a typical middle game situation.

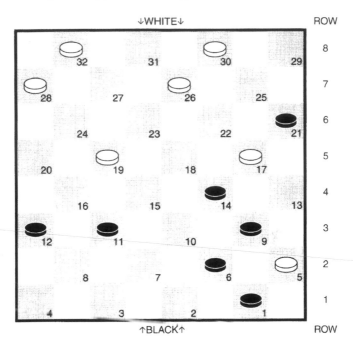

Diagram 19

A late-stage middle game layout. Each player has seven checkers and what appear to be evenly positioned armies. It's black's turn and he makes some masterful moves to take the lead and win the game. What are they?

Finally, there's the endgame when both players have fewer forces, but usually some kings, and they are battling each other for superiority in manpower and/or a dominating position that will lead to victory. Diagram 20 pictures an endgame about to be ended.

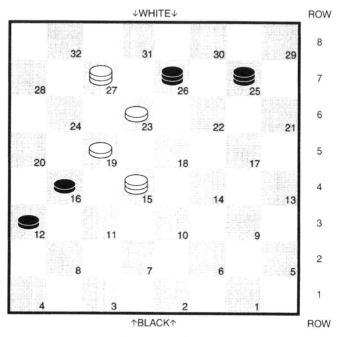

Diagram 20

In this endgame both players have equivalent forces. It's white's turn to go, and what a go he makes of it to win the contest with a couple of great moves that are capped by a spectacular jumping sequence. How does white do it?

A checker game can be won or lost in any of these three phases, as indicated in the diagram captions. As soon as a player has lost a checker without getting an immediate reciprocal jumping capture, he is in trouble. The opponent, being one piece ahead, can try to exchange checkers, one-for-one or two-for-two, in a series of even trade-offs, as long as they don't compromise his strategic position. If the player who is one piece ahead can carry out this swapping approach with all the remaining checker pieces, he will win—one to none! Diagram 21 illustrates this "grind-'em-down" ploy.

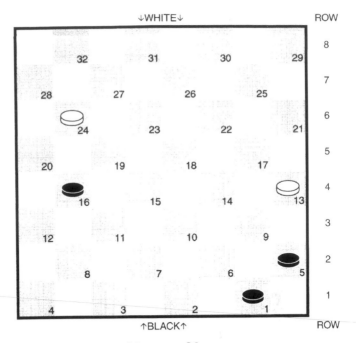

Diagram 21

Here it's black's move. He's ahead in checker power, three to two. He finds a game-winning two-for-two trade that prevents white from getting any kings and prolonging the agony. Do you see how he does it?

Before delving into the specific considerations involved with each of these three phases of the game, numerous tactics and strategies that apply to two or all three of the segments need to be examined. These are of critical importance, regardless of how many moves and jumps have been made.

Thinking Ahead

The most important stratagem of all in checkers is succinctly stated in the slogan made famous by IBM's founding president, Thomas Watson, who coined the wonderfully instructive phrase "Think." While Watson was advocating this thought process for business purposes, it is also the paramount principle to heed for anyone who wants to play a good game of checkers with a realistic chance of winning. "Think ahead" is an even better credo for checkers because the player who doesn't think carefully about what can happen after he moves is quite likely to make a bad move or miss out on a much better one. It's very important to take your time, have a reason for every move, consider as many viable alternatives as you can find, and figure out what your opponent might do after you move and what you'll be able to do after that. This is especially significant with the single checker pieces that can never retreat to a safer or better position since they, unlike the kings, can move only forward. The late Dr. Marion Tinsley, the greatest checker player the world has ever known, said, "Checkers is essentially a test of what you can see, not what you know." Diagram 22 makes Tinsley's point.

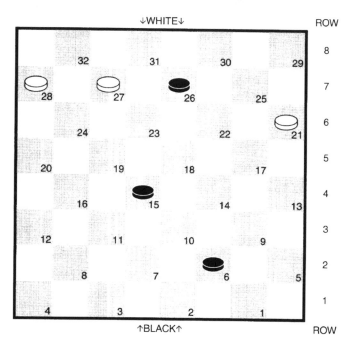

Diagram 22

It's black's move. He's done very well to get a checker all the way to 26 where it can be converted to a king on this move. If black thinks carefully about his move into the king row, he will have an excellent chance of winning. If he doesn't think ahead, there's a good possibility that he could move and lose. What should black do and why?

Controlling the Center

Fighting for control of the center of the board (squares 14, 15, 18, and 19) provides players with twice as many opportunities for future moves than they would have by moving to momentary safety on the sides of the board (squares 13 and 20). The checkers in the middle can move and jump in two directions, whereas those on the side can move or jump only one way (toward the middle). The kings' options also double when they are in the middle rather than on the perimeter squares—they have four possibilities from a central location, but can move or jump in only two directions from the sides or ends of the board. These positional pros and cons are depicted in Diagram 23.

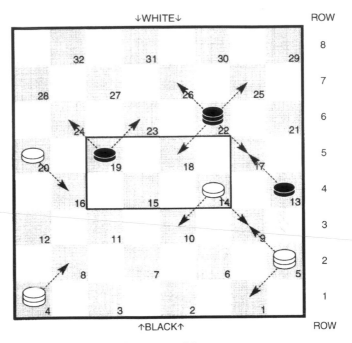

Diagram 23

The checkers on squares 13 and 20 can move only one way (to 17 and 16 respectively). They can jump only one way (to 22 and 11 respectively). The checkers in the middle (on squares 14 and 19) can move and/or jump in two directions. The black king on square 22 can move and/or jump in four directions. The white kings on the perimeter squares (4 and 5) are much more severely restricted in their movements.

It is more dangerous to be on the center squares because the pieces there can be jumped while the checkers and kings on the perimeter squares cannot except via a sacrificial exchange. These risks are more than offset by the much greater flexibility of movement available to the pieces in the middle, in comparison to the safer but more restrictive positions on the boundary squares.

Looking for Multiple-Jumping Opportunities

Finding multiple-jumping opportunities (double jumps, triple jumps, etc.) can often win a game for the cautiously aggressive player who gives up one or two pieces to set up a reciprocating jumping sequence that enables him to capture more of the opponent's pieces in return. These favorable exchanges almost always provide the multiple jumper with a vastly improved position on the board as well. Conversely, a key defensive strategy is to vigilantly guard against putting your pieces in positions where they are exposed to multiple jumps by the opponent. The multiple jumps that start with a sacrificial move are called shots. Two examples of these shots are shown and described in Diagrams 24 and 25.

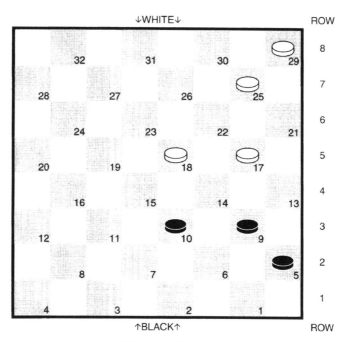

Diagram 24

It's black's turn to go with a one-checker deficit. He finds a game-winning shot that is sparked with the sacrifice of the checker on square 9 by moving it to 14. White has to jump from 18 to 9 and give black's checker on 5 a victorious triple leap into the king row from 5 to 14 to 21 to 30. White could have won this game by avoiding anything worse than an even exchange.

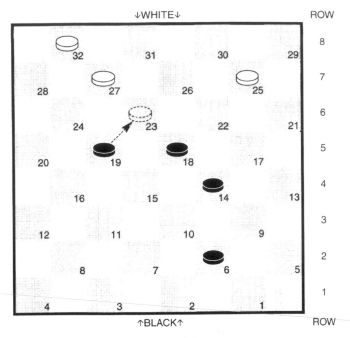

				ROW
32	31	30	29	8
28	27	26	25	7
24	23	22	21	6
20	19	18	17	5
16	15	14	13	4
12	11	10	9	3
8	7	6	5	2
4	3	2	1	1

Diagram 25

Black is leading four to three. He's so anxious to get a king that he doesn't think ahead, and moves from 19 to 23, which looks like a fast, safe route into the king row. It isn't! White plays a deadly shot, sacrificing from 25 to 22. Black must jump from 18 to 25 and give white a triple jump from 27 to 18 to 9 to 2. White's new king will be able to trap black on one of the perimeter squares in no more than five moves. Had black moved from 6 to 9 at the outset, he could have easily won this match.

Protecting the King Row

Making it difficult for the opponent to move or jump into his king row (the defender's back row) is a vitally important defensive tactic in order to avoid all the dangerous threats that are posed by these powerful "Monarchs of the Squares." Some novice players carry this tactic to an unrewarding and disastrous extreme by steadfastly refusing to leave their back row, on the mistaken theory that as long as they have their pieces on the four squares there, the opponent cannot get in. This entrenchment strategy prevents them from properly supporting their other checkers as they move them up the board. It does not prevent the opponent from getting into the king row, as shown in Diagram 26, with black gaining access to the king row and a crown via a one-for-one exchange. The king row can be adequately protected with only two of the four back row checkers remaining on their starting squares, while the other two move out to work with the rest of their forces as they attack the opponent's back row so they can get in there to crown some kings.

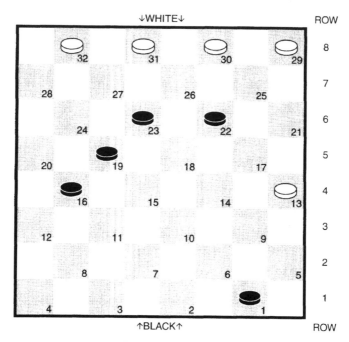

Diagram 26

This shows white entrenched in the back row. Black has positioned his checkers to gain entry by exchanging 23 to 26, and after white jumps from 30 to 23, black jumps right back from 19 to 26 and will get a king on his next move. White hasn't developed any support for his checker on 13 and he faces a very difficult task in the moves ahead, as black's king will terrorize the white checkers from behind. Black should win from here with careful play.

Although getting a king is usually very advantageous, situations arise where the opponent can use his adversary's new king to seriously damage the enemy by forcing the new monarch to jump on his next move right after it is crowned by setting up a retaliatory jumping play that wipes out the new king and, quite often, some other pieces as well. This double-edged-sword strategy was shown in Diagram 22 and is also depicted in Diagrams 47, 48, and 62.

How to Leave the King Row (Back Row)

Although only two checkers are needed to stand guard in the back row, it's crucial to know who should stay and who should go when vacating this area. The best checker to move out first is usually the one in the single corner (square 4 for black and square 29 for white), because even after these checkers have left their initial positions for assignments further up the board, it is still very difficult for the opponent to move into those corners. Black must position a piece on square 21 and white on square 12 in order to get safely into the single corner. It can also be difficult to get a new king back out of that corner and into play. A white checker on square 26 or a black piece on square 7 can prevent a newly crowned black or white king from making a safe departure. Diagram 27 shows how leaving the single corner in the back row does very little harm to the defender's position.

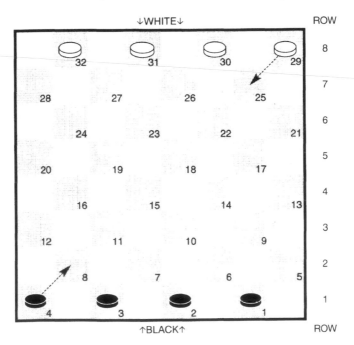

Diagram 27

Arrows indicate what are usually the best checkers for black and white to move first when they are leaving their back row (the opponent's king row) to support their checkers that are further up the board. Even after these single corner checkers have departed, it's still hard for an enemy piece to get into and out of these isolated squares.

The next or second best checker for the defender to move out of the king row has to be determined in conjunction with the way the game is developing. If your double corner is under a serious attack, it's a good strategy to keep the checkers on squares 1 and 5 for black and 28 and 32 for white in place as long as possible. This can thwart an opponent's thrust in that direction. In these cases, the second best checker to move out of the back row is from square 2 for black and square 31 for white because, even after they are gone, it's still hard for the opponent to move into his king row. Black would have to post a piece on square 23 in order to slide safely in and white would have to do the same on square 10. These access routes are not as cloistered as the single corner, because there are two pathways into these empty squares, as well as two alternative exits for the new king to choose from as he returns to the fray. The single corner, as previously discussed, offers only one way in and one way out. This makes it much more restrictive to the opponent's movements. Diagram 28 illustrates this type of departure from the back row. This assumes the single corner checker had already left, earlier in the game, which is most often the case.

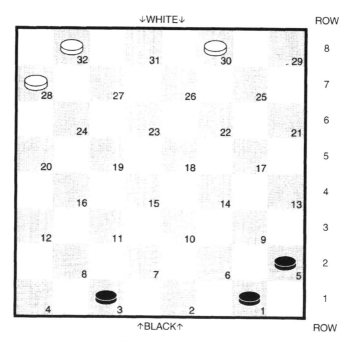

Diagram 28

Black and white are staunchly defending their back rows by vacating the middle squares in these rows (2 for black and 31 for white). Black will have to post a piece on square 21 or 23 and white on 10 or 12 in order to get safely into and out of their respective king rows.

If the other player has turned his attack away from the double corner, it's usually a good idea to keep the triangle formation created by the checkers on squares 2, 3, and 7 (for black) and squares 26, 30, and 31 (for white) intact. Together, these three pieces represent a formidable defense. This strategy will eventually require a move out of the double corner from square 1 for black or from square 32 for white. In these situations, the checker on the other double-corner square (5 for black and 28 for white) should be maintained in place, if possible, because its presence on this square, in concert with those in the back row, still makes it hard for the opponent to penetrate into the king row. If both of the double-corner checkers are missing in action, the other player will have easy access to the king row. Diagram 29 shows this solid defensive position for black. It's also obvious that either of the white checkers on squares 13 or 14 would have easy, unchallenged access to their king row in three more moves (from 13 or 14 to 9 to 5 to 1) if square 5 were unoccupied.

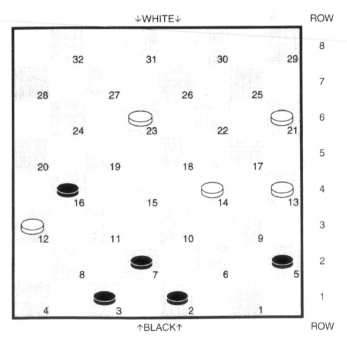

Diagram 29

Black is shown maintaining a solid defensive formation on squares 2, 3, and 7, while his checker on square 5 still makes it difficult for white to get into the king row. If the black checker on square 5 weren't there, white could move either of his checkers from squares 13 or 14 into the king row in three uncontested moves: to 9 to 5 to 1.

In most situations the back-row checker in the double corner (square 1 for black and square 32 for white) is the worst checker to move out early in the game. Once this checker is gone, the opponent can launch an attack on the double corner with the objective of forcing the other guardian (on square 5 for black and on square 28 for white) out of its protective post via a one-for-one jumping exchange. If this is done, the opponent will have clear sailing into the king row as discussed and illustrated immediately above in Diagram 29.

Using Kings as Soon as Possible

Because of the king's awesome power, it should be put into play as soon after being crowned as possible. While this seems like an obviously sensible tactic, many novice players go on a quest to get as many kings as they can before moving any of them back into the battle. They do this because they think they will be stronger and better able to successfully attack the enemy with an army dominated by kings than they would be with just one. But one lone king on the loose can put a great deal of pressure on the other player, who will have a very hard time escaping from the enemy monarch's multi-directional moving and jumping capabilities. If the first crowned king is held in reserve until others are anointed, the unthreatened opponent will probably be able to secure some kings of his own, leading to a long, drawn-out contest and very possibly a tie game. Diagram 30 illustrates this point.

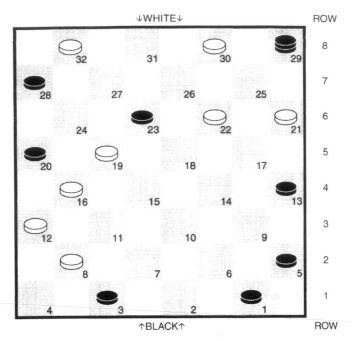

Diagram 30

Black has a newly crowned king on square 29 and it's black's turn. Moving the king right out to 25 will put a lot of pressure on white, and black should be able to win. If, instead, he moves his checker on square 20 to 24 to get another king, white will also be able to get some kings that will put the game in limbo. In this diagram, if black didn't move his king out immediately, white could trap him in the single corner by going from 21 to 17.

Offensive and Defensive Considerations

Checker games have been compared to a battle between opposing armies with the checkers as foot soldiers and the kings as the "big guns." Just as a good general keeps his supply lines intact during a war, it's vitally important to be conservative with your forces and to protect the integrity of your support system as you move toward your king row. It's a tactical mistake to move one or two of your checkers up the board so far and so fast that they are put in a position where they are vulnerable to an enemy attack without an adequate defense, because the opponent may very well be able to capture them in a one-for-none exchange as depicted in Diagram 31. Checker champion Tom Wiswell said, "Moves that disturb your position the least, disturb the opposition the most."

47

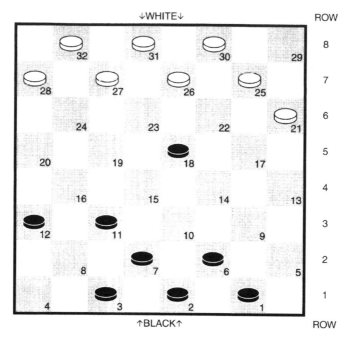

Diagram 31

A positional setup after black has made eight moves and white has had seven turns. Black's checker on 18 has strayed too far ahead of his troop's defensive range and is vulnerable to a pick-off attack by white, who moves from 26 to 23. Black's most strenuous response to this threat (B 1–5, W 23–14, B 6–9, W 30–26, B 9–18, W 26–23, B 2–6, W 23–14, B 6–9, W 31–26, B 9–18, W 26–23) cannot stop white from going a checker up in manpower, with a positional advantage as well, for a likely win.

In the early game and through at least the first half of the middle game, it can be very dangerous to have one or two of your checkers much further ahead on the board than those of your opponent, as shown above. Later in the middle game and in the endgame, the situation changes, and the pieces that have been moved carefully forward toward their king row should now have some good opportunities to get their crowns and wreak havoc. An example of this carefully aggressive positioning is shown in Diagram 32.

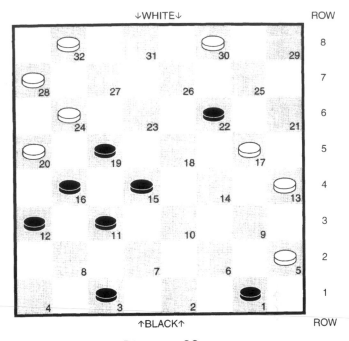

	ROW
32 31 30 29	8
28 27 26 25	7
24 23 22 21	6
20 19 18 17	5
16 15 14 13	4
12 11 10 9	3
8 7 6 5	2
4 3 2 1	1

Diagram 32

A late middle game in which black has moved to square 22 to pin the white checker on 30 without putting himself in any jeopardy. Now black can get an early king via an even exchange by moving from 22 to 26 and forcing white to jump from 30 to 23. Black gets a reciprocal jump from 19 to 26 and can move into his king row whenever it's propitious.

Although winning the game is the first priority, a tie, while not as satisfying as a win, is obviously much better than a loss. Successful players usually think and move in ways that help to ensure themselves of a draw in the event that their efforts to lure the opponent into a trap do not work. Instead of taking dramatic risks that could cause them to lose the game if they backfire, they make cautiously aggressive moves that provide them with a realistic chance of winning, while still being able to fall back to a drawing strategy, depending on what moves the opponent makes. Diagram 33 shows an example of black making an assertive move that, with the slightest miscue on white's part, holds out some excellent winning possibilities, without compromising black's chances to defend his position and redirect his attack.

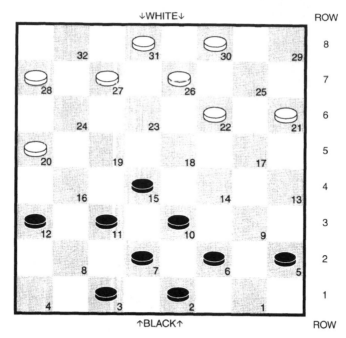

| | | 8 |
| 32 | 31 | 30 | 29 |

(board positions)

Diagram 33

Black has control of the center with a solid formation and it's his turn. Black makes a cautiously aggressive play from 15 to 19. If white goes from 27 to 24, black will move from 3 to 8 and get a double jump from 11 to 18 to 25 after white jumps from 24 to 15. If white moves one of his men on 21 or 22, black will go from 19 to 24 to set up a triple jump into his king row after white jumps from 28 to 19. Black would do this by sacrificing 11 to 16 and after white jumped from 20 to 11, black would leap from 7 to 16 to 23 to 32. If white doesn't fall into either of these traps, black will still be in a strong position to look for and launch an alternative attack.

Looking for Breeches (and Looking Out for Them)

Checker breeches often present a surefire capturing opportunity for an alert player with a properly positioned king. A breech is formed by two same-color checker pieces (kings can be included), on the same diagonal line, one square apart, with empty, unprotected squares on the same diagonal line in the row immediately ahead of the forward piece and in the row right behind the other, as pictured in Diagram 34. If an opponent can move into the breech with a king, he will, on his next turn, jump the piece that was not moved, or whichever one he wants to if both have been left in place because his adversary chose to move another piece.

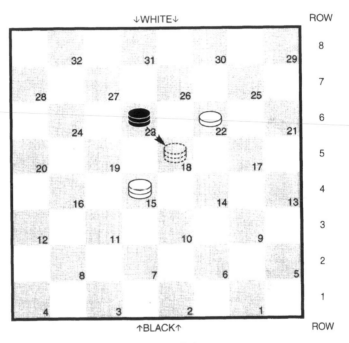

Diagram 34

It's black's turn to go and he'll move right into the breech created by white's king on 15 and white's checker on 22. No matter which one of these pieces white moves, black will get a game-tying jump!

Avoiding the Doghole

Squares 5 for white and 28 for black are called the dogholes, because checkers on these squares are immobilized as long as the opponent keeps his checker on the other double corner square in his back row (squares 1 and 32). The player with a checker in the doghole is at the mercy of the opponent (and most show none), since he can't move that piece until the opponent vacates the other double corner square. This gives the enemy a strong upper hand. Diagram 35 shows how being in the doghole results in a loss for black, in spite of the fact that both sides have an equal number of checkers.

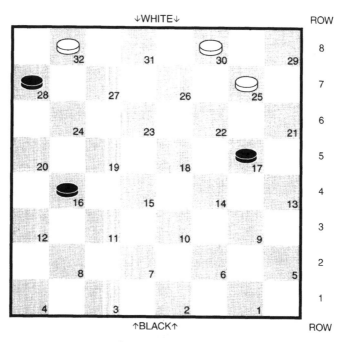

Diagram 35

Although both players have three checkers apiece, one of black's is immobilized in the doghole on square 28 by white's checker on 32, while white can move any one of his three men. If it were white's turn, he'd exchange one for one by moving from 25 to 22 and forcing black to jump from 17 to 26. White would jump back from 30 to 23 and black would have to move from 16 to 20. From there, black would have to give the white checker on 32 a jump in two more moves. If it were black's turn in the position shown, he would have to move either 16 to 20 or 17 to 21 (if he went 16 to 19, white would get a game-winning double jump by sacrificing 25 to 22), which would result in a similar win for white.

Perseverance Pays Off

Perseverance is probably the second most important trait (next to thinking ahead) that every good checker player needs to succeed in games against serious opponents. Many games have been tied, or even won, by the player who would not give up too easily. Sometimes when an opponent gets ahead in checker power and/or position, the other player resigns himself to losing and surrenders prematurely. In other cases, players at a disadvantage become discouraged, lose interest, play listlessly, and are inevitably defeated. But the resilient competitor, even if he's behind, continues to think things through. He looks for opportunities to reverse a manpower deficit. He tries to find ways to extricate himself from a weakened position. These persistent efforts can often prove to be very successful, which encourages more of the same. And remember: sometimes opponents, having taken the lead, tend to relax a little, let down their guard, and, with a false sense of security, make a mistake that helps turn the tide of battle in favor of the underdog who wouldn't quit. Diagram 36 depicts such a case.

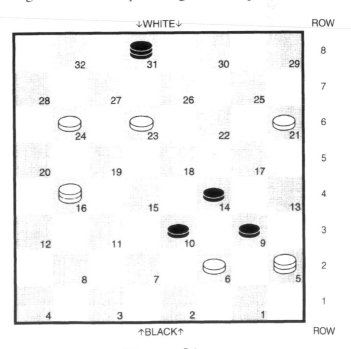

Diagram 36

It's black's move. He has a serious manpower shortage and a seemingly disastrous positional problem. Instead of giving up, black searches for and finds a way to win the game in three moves. There's nothing white can do to stop him! Can you find black's winning plays?

However, there are times where the situation really is hopeless, as previously shown in Diagrams 14 and 15. Surrendering in those situations saves time and shows intellectual courtesy to the opponent who would have to make almost unthinkable errors to lose or tie.

Simultaneous Sacrificing

Simultaneously offering the opponent two alternative jumping opportunities in order to force his pieces into a vulnerable position while allowing time to move one of your pieces to a square that takes full advantage of the newly manipulated layout is a strategic ploy (as shown in Diagram 36) that doesn't come up very often. But it is worth looking for because, when it is discovered, it can spell instant gratification, as is seen again in Diagram 39.

Opening and Early Game Considerations

Black always starts the game and sets the tone by his first move. The strongest opening move for black is to go from square 11 to 15. This puts him in the center of the board and facilitates an early departure from the single corner (square 4) when that play becomes advisable. The second-best opening is from 9 to 14, which is also in the middle. It does nothing to free up the checker on square 4, nor does it obstruct it. The moves 10 to 15 and 11 to 16 are in a dead heat for the third-best opening. The former is right in the center, but it creates another obstacle in terms of being able to move from 4 to 8 later on in the game. The latter is still near the center and does help to make way for the 4-to-8 play. Next, or fifth-best, is 10 to 14, which lets white get a good start on controlling the center. The move 12 to 16 ranks sixth—it's at least moving toward the middle, but it makes it easy for white to get control of this key area. The very worst opening move is, ironically, the most popular one of all the possibilities with almost every beginner or infrequent player. The novice invariably goes from square 9 to 13 for safety's sake, since you can't be jumped when you are on the sideline squares. This play immediately relinquishes the center to white and does nothing to provide for black's development out of the single corner. The seven opening moves are listed below in order of preference and are also shown in Diagram 37.

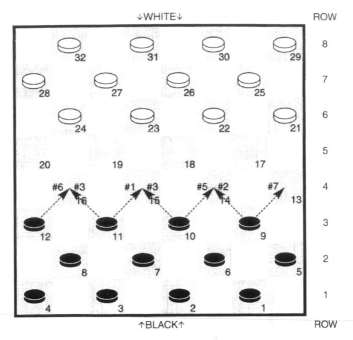

Diagram 37

The arrows and numbers illustrate the best (#1) to the worst (#7) opening moves for black in a Go As You Please (GAYP) game. Note that 10 to 15 and 11 to 16 are considered to be equal in strength as the third-best opening moves.

Best 11–15
2nd 9–14
3rd 10–15 and 11–16 (equal in strength)
5th 10–14
6th 12–16
Worst 9–13

White's responses to each of these black initiatives follow a similar pattern of rationale. White should fight for control of the center squares and try to prepare for a move out of his single corner (from square 29 to 25). He should also avoid the debilitating move to the side (24 to 20). It is the weakest move he could make no matter where black goes to start, for the same reasons cited for black's moving from 9 to 13. During the first few salvos, each player fights for control of the middle, defends his front-line checkers, looks for (and guards against) double- and triple-jumping opportunities, while striving to prevent the opponent from gaining access to the king row.

Since the 11-to-15 opening is recognized by every experienced

55

player as the very strongest for black, everyone with any real knowledge of the game usually makes this move to lead off. In Go As You Please (GAYP) games, which are games in which both players can make whatever legal moves they want, white's best replies are 23 to 19 (also in the center) and 22 to 18, forcing black to jump from 15 to 22, which gives white momentary control of the center with a jump back from 25 to 18.

In order to generate a more interesting pattern of play among serious checker enthusiasts, a three-move ballot is often used, especially in tournaments. There are 130 of these three-move cards that note a required first move for both black and white along with black's second move. One of these cards listing the first three moves (such as Black 9–14, White 22–17, Black 5–9) is drawn by black and shared with white. These first three restrictive moves are made automatically. Then white makes a move of his own choosing. Black responds with his choice and the game is on.

All sorts of opportunities develop for an alert player in the early stages of play. There might be a chance to get a checker or two ahead with a sacrifice move (a shot) that leads to a double or triple jump, a better position on the board, and an eventual win. You may be able to force or draw your opponent out of his double corner, which could make it easier to get a king there. Possibilities arise that enable carefully aggressive players to dominate the center of the board where they have more attacking options than their opponents. On the other side of the coin, there are always risks of making an ill-considered move that would allow the opponent to make a gain in material, positioning, or both. It's never too early to try to get a defendable checker on square 19 (for black) or 14 (for white). From there it may be possible to formulate and launch a successful assault on the opponent's double corner during the middle game and obtain a valuable king relatively early in the contest.

Diagrams 38 to 42 depict five early game situations taken from actual matches. Each of these provides opportunities for the resourceful player to gain a winning advantage in manpower and/or position by thinking ahead and moving accordingly. As you search through these problems to find the right solutions, you will be well on your way to becoming a very capable early-game player. There remain a goodly number of careful moves that would need to be made by the player with the upper hand to actually win these games. A simple mistake, in what might be looked upon as a mopping-up exercise, could still result in a tie or even a loss. In checkers, the price of success is constant vigilance. If you can't solve these puzzles after some careful study, you can consult and learn from the answers in the solution section on page 98.

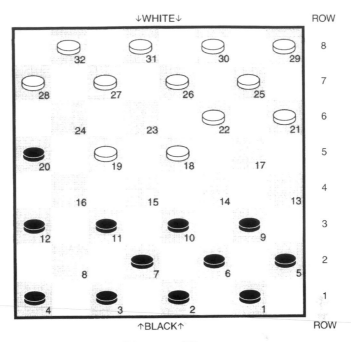

Diagram 38

In this innocent-looking early game, it's white's move, and what a move he makes! It triggers a world series of jumps that leaves white about to get a king and a piece ahead. White should be able to win from here. What is white's first move and how does he follow it up?

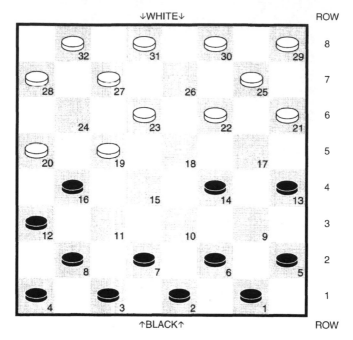

Diagram 39

Each player has made just three moves and white's checker on 20 is threatening to jump the black checker on 16. Black turns this problem into a game-winning opportunity with a surprising response that gains him a king and a two-piece lead. What does black do and what happens afterward?

58

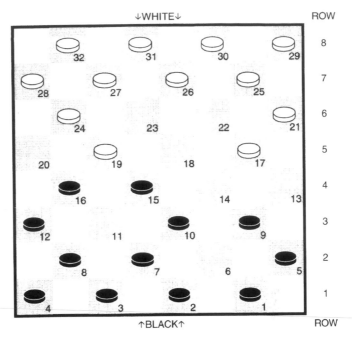

Diagram 40

There haven't been any exchanges in this early game. It's white's move and he uses black's attack on the white checker on 19 to great advantage with a devastating play that leads to a triple jump, a white king, and an almost certain victory! Can you figure out how white does all this?

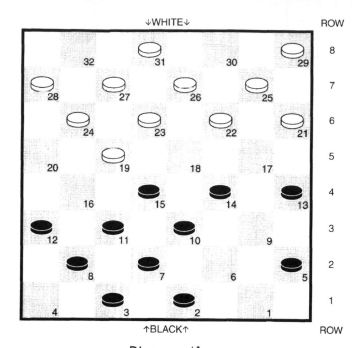

Diagram 41

Both sides have eleven checkers and it's white's turn. He puts it to great use with a neat combination play that opens up a pathway to glory. What did white see and do?

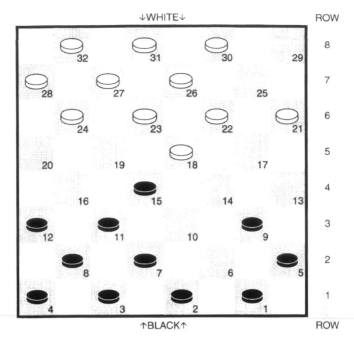

Diagram 42

This appears to be an even start for both sides. It's black's move and he proves that appearances can be deceiving by making some strategic plays to go a checker up and almost get a king. What's his strategy?

Middle Game Opportunities

The middle game is a thought-provoking and pivotal point in a checker contest after 10 or so moves have been made by each player. While most new checker fans think of the endgame as the grand finale, many knowledgeable players consider the middle game to be the most important because it so often is the determining factor in the end result. A bad move here could definitely lose the game. A continuing series of average efforts by both sides is likely to bring about a draw. But well-thought-out, innovative, strategic play at this time in the match could spell victory. If the contest looks just about equal at this juncture, it's probably because the players are evenly matched. Now it's up to one or the other to come up with some above-average moves that will put him in the driver's seat. Remember to continue your fight for control of the center and to protect your back row against the opponent's campaign to get a king. If black's attempts to put a securely defended checker on square 19 have been successful (white's intermediate goal is to do the same on square 14), he should continue thrusting at the double

61

corner. In order to parry such an attack, the opponent may marshal too many of his men on that side of the board, thereby depleting his lineup on the other half. If that happens, the offense should be redirected to that area, the single corner section, where there is less resistance. Diagram 43 relates to these strategic considerations and maneuvers.

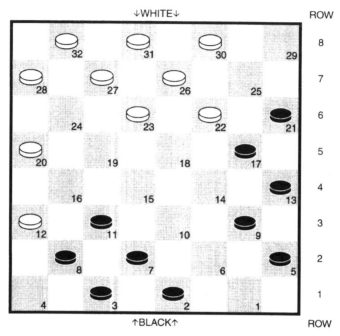

Diagram 43

White has stymied black's thrust at the double corner by stationing a lot of his men in that area. Black turns his attention to the other side (the single corner) and finds a fast lane into his king row by using an imaginative two-for-two jumping exchange. He sacrifices 21 to 25, and white has to double-jump from 30 to 21 to 14. Black double-jumps right back from 9 to 18 to 25. He'll get an uncontested king on his next move. Where there's a will, there's a way!

Through at least the first half of the middle game, it's good strategy to keep your men compactly intact as you move them up the board. But as you drive closer and closer to the king row, it may be necessary and safer to move one or two of the more advanced men a row ahead of the pack (to row 6 for black and to 3 for white) where they are threatening to gain access to the king row without being put into harm's way. From these aggressive positions they may also be able to pin the opponent's back-row checkers in place, so as to make it difficult for them to get out to support their compatriots. This is illustrated in Diagram 44.

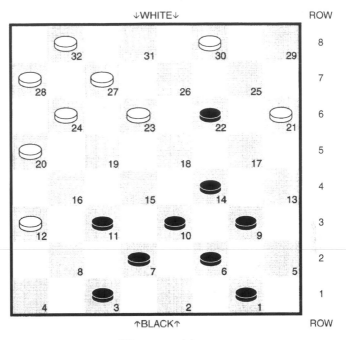

Diagram 44

In this late middle game, black has kept his checkers close together as they've worked their way up the board. Now he's seen an opportunity to pin the white checker on 30 and has moved two rows in front of the rest of his forces to accomplish this. He's not in any danger there now and he can get an early king at his discretion.

The following middle game puzzles (again, taken from actual playing circumstances) will require the problem-solver to keep his thinking cap on. They can all be won by some adroit moves, but timing is everything here. If the right move isn't made at the very moment shown in Diagrams 45 to 49, the opponent may very well slip away to do some serious damage of his own. The answers are in the aforementioned solution section, but don't refer to them until you've given each of these a good mental whirl. Use a numbered checkerboard and checkers to set up the situations and to experiment with the possibilities—it will be a big help.

Seize the moment!

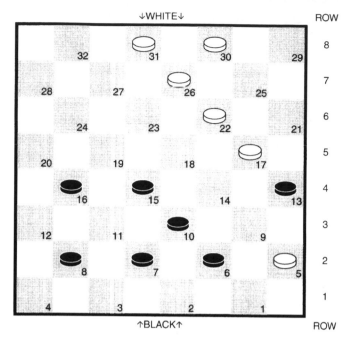

Here it's white's turn in a late-stage middle game. He's trailing by one checker, but is about to get a king that could do a lot of damage to the opposition. Instead of going right in for the crown, though, white makes three completely unexpected sacrifices that set up a mind-boggling jumping sequence to sink the black ship. How does he navigate this treacherous course?

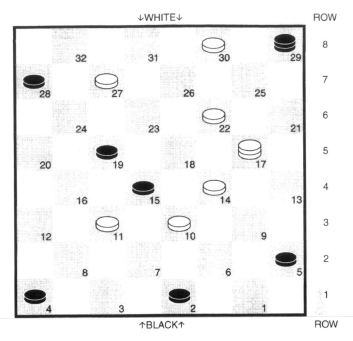

Diagram 46

Shown here is a late-phase middle game with equal troop strength including a king for each side, although black's king is momentarily trapped in a single corner. It's white's move and the one he selects starts a chain reaction that results in a brilliant triumph. What are the moves?

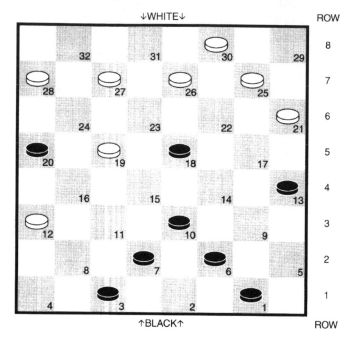

Diagram 47

Here's another evenly matched middle game with black to move. It doesn't look like either side has any real advantage until black, who sees things differently, makes some startling plays that lead to a victory celebration. How does he do it?

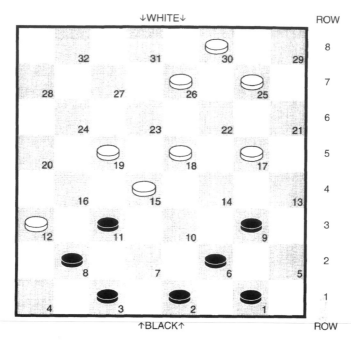

Diagram 48

It's black's move and he's outgunned by white—eight to seven—in this middle game. But he employs some black magic to chalk up a sensational win. What's his secret strategy?

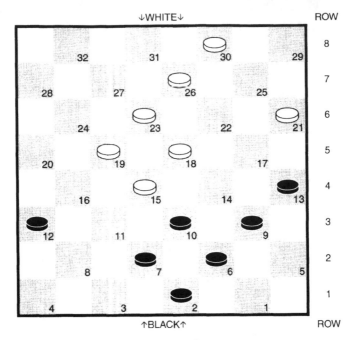

Diagram 49

A late middle-game illustration with seven men left for each side. It's black's play and his prospects do not look promising. But he makes the most out of this dire-straits situation and sails home with a gratifying triumph! Can you find the course that black took?

The Challenging Endgame

The endgame is always exciting, at least for the winner, and also for the player who ties by making a successful comeback from what looked like a probable loss. There are fewer pieces on the board at this stage, so there is more room for moves and jumps. Both players are likely to have kings by this time, which creates more opportunities for offensive and defensive play, as well as more danger. If there is ever a time to play with extra caution, this is it! How can you get more of your checkers into the king row without having them captured or trapped on the sides of the board? What can you do to stop your opponent from converting his checkers into kings? Can you find a way to immobilize all the other player's pieces? Are there any setups where you could finish things off with a shot-ignited multiple jump? Does it look like it's going to be a tie game? The answers to all these and more questions will help to determine what your most effective endgame strategy is or how it needs to be readjusted. One of the reasons that checkers is so fascinating is because it's so dynamic!

This is a good time to try to force your opponent to move to the side of the board, where his pieces will be more restricted. If you are ahead in manpower, look for even exchanges or, better yet, try to trade one of your checkers for an opponent's king. Now, more than ever, these kinds of swaps can win the game. If you are behind, avoid the one-for-one trade-off. Get as many kings as you can, even if it means letting your opponent get more too. Three kings versus four is a much better ratio for the player on the defensive than two versus three or one versus two. The latter two combinations usually result in certain defeat for the player who is at a deficit.

Many casual players do not know how to use a one-king-up advantage (2 vs. 1, 3 vs. 2, and 4 vs. 3) to bring about a victory that should be rightfully theirs once they have achieved this numerical superiority. The winning strategy in these cases is to first reduce the ratio in the higher number combinations to the 2-to-1 level with even exchanges (usually one-for-one). At that point, the player with two kings chases his opponent's solo monarch into one of the double corners (if the lone king goes anywhere else, he will be easily trapped somewhere on the perimeter). From that location, the series of winning moves for the aggressor always follows an identical pattern, although the squares involved will be different depending on the double corner where the play takes place and which square in the corner has to be vacated by the lone king. An example of the procedure required to force the opponent into giving up his last king is shown below and described with notations in Diagram 50.

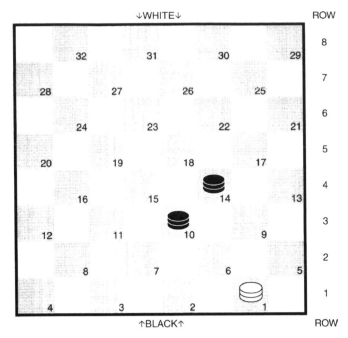

↑BLACK↑   ROW

Diagram 50

A typical two-king-against-one-king ending. Black's first objective is to drive white's lone king out of the double corner. He starts by moving 14 to 9, and white has to go 1 to 5. Black moves 10 to 14, so white must move 5 to 1. Black zips into the double corner with 9 to 5, forcing white out from 1 to 6. Now black goes 5 to 1 and white's only safe move is from 6 to 2. Then black retreats momentarily from 14 to 18,* but white can only go 2 to 7. Black goes back on the attack with 18 to 15, and white must move back to either 2 or 3. After white moves to one of these squares, black slides from 15 to 11 and it's all over.

*The 14-to-18 move for black is the key to winning. If black had moved 14 to 10 at that point, white could go from 2 to 6 for a seesawing continuation and a possible tie if black couldn't find the winning formula.

With three kings against two, the strategy is to reduce the ratio to two versus one with an even exchange. This may be easier said than done, especially if the player with the two kings has one in each of the two double corners where they can move back and forth as well as in and out to try to avoid the trade-off attempts that are being made by the numerically superior opponent. Novice players often become so frustrated by their inability to accomplish the required exchange that they offer to call the match a draw, which is eagerly accepted by the relieved underdog. This is always a mistake, since the one-for-one exchange cannot be denied if the offense makes the proper sequence of moves, as depicted and discussed in Diagram 51 below.

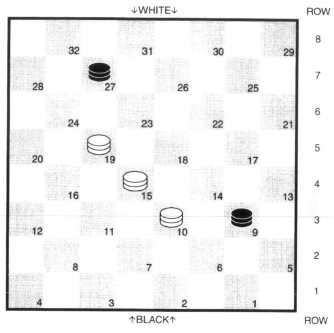

Diagram 51

Here we have three white kings lined up to force black into an even exchange so that the two-against-one strategic maneuvers explained in Diagram 50 can be carried out to a winning conclusion. White starts with 15 to 18, and black must move back into one of the double corners. He picks 27 to 32, and white goes 19 to 24. Black has to reply 9 to 5 (32 to 28 would give white an even exchange with 18 to 15). White moves 10 to 14, and black must go 32 to 28 to avoid a trade (white would sacrifice 24 to 27 if black stayed on 32). Next, white moves 24 to 27 and it's almost over. If black moves 28 to 32, white will reply 27 to 23 and get the trade on his following turn. Should black play 5 to 1, white would respond with 14 to 9 and get the even exchange by backing up the king on square 18 with his king that is not being threatened. While the sequence of moves will vary in accordance with the starting positions and the disadvantaged player's choice of moves, the winning pattern of forcing plays is always identical and well worth learning.

In other situations, where a player is a king ahead (4 to 3, 5 to 4, etc.), this same careful swapping technique should enable him to reduce the ratio to two against one. At this point, if the opponent is an experienced player, he will probably resign in the face of certain defeat. Otherwise the inevitable victory can be achieved by simply repeating the routine movements as stipulated in Diagram 50.

Many endgames boil down to a situation in which one player has two kings and the other has one king and a checker. The player with two kings can win many of these endings if he can stop the opponent from moving his checker into the king row (which would probably result in a draw) while forcing the solo king out of the double corner and into jeopardy. Then the opponent will have to move his checker from a safe perimeter square to a more vulnerable position toward the center, where he can be subjected to capture. After that is done, some careful play designed to trap the opposition or to lure him into an even swap that creates a winning position can bring about a well-deserved victory. A classic example of this type of an endgame is illustrated in Diagram 52, which also includes a description of the specific series of moves that must be made to win. This sort of setup happens so often, with some slight positional variations, that it is considered to be a standard endgame pattern and, as such, is often referred to in checker literature as First Position. If you study and learn the proper sequence of moves to make in these circumstances, it will improve your understanding of endgame tactics and your win-loss record. Following the annotated moves by actually making them on a numbered board will greatly facilitate your understanding.

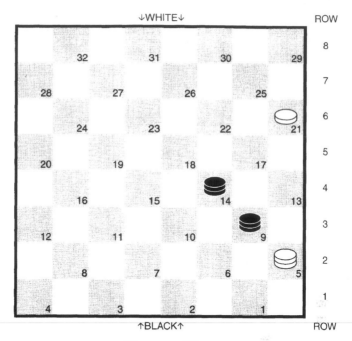

Diagram 52

This is the classic First Position, with the annotated moves required for black to move and win. One false step can let white off the hook and into a tie, if white gets a second king. Numerous variations of First Position play are generated by the starting location of the pieces and the defensive player's moves. The aggressor's moves all relate to the core strategy of forcing the opponent's lone king out of the double corner and into jeopardy. Then the checker on the perimeter square has to leave its safe haven and be subjected to capture. An annotation from the position shown is listed below:

Black	White		Black	White
1. 9–6	5–1	8. 5–1	6–9
2. 14–10	1–5	9. 15–18	9–5
3. 6–1	5–9	10. 18–22	17–14
4. 10–15	9–5	11. 1–6	5–1
5. 15–18	5–9	12. 6–2	14–10
6. 1–5	9–6	13. 22–18	1– 5
7. 18–15	21–17	14. 18–14	Black wins

There are four additional endgame configurations that come into play so often that they too are familiar standards. As such, they have been imaginatively named Second, Third, Fourth, and Fifth Positions.

In each, a precise series of the moves required to win have been analytically worked out by checker experts. If these sequences are flawlessly duplicated by the advantaged player, they will lead to a laborious but gratifying victory. One slip along the way can give the underdog a much-sought-after draw. These four positions are diagrammed with their annotated solutions beginning on page 103. Serious students of the game will find it productive to spend time learning about each. This effort will be especially rewarding when confronted with these offensive and defensive positions, from either end of the board, in a game.

Endgame Blocks
Although the opportunity to immobilize the other player's pieces so they can't move or jump anywhere when it's his turn can arise before the endgame, it is a real rarity. And, while the chance to do this doesn't come up very often in the endgame either, the possibility does present itself more often than it does earlier, especially if you consider the checker that is stuck in the doghole with no place to go when all the other checkers and kings have been captured as being blocked (technically, it is). The alert player looks for ways to make this startling, winning ending happen toward the late stages of a match and also guards against letting himself fall into such a debilitating loss. If you can make one of these immobilizing plays against an unwary opponent, you can win what looked like a lost cause. Conversely, you certainly don't want to be lured into one of these deadly pitfalls. Diagram 53 shows an example of black's manipulating an unsuspecting competitor (who was well ahead) into this most exasperating defeat.

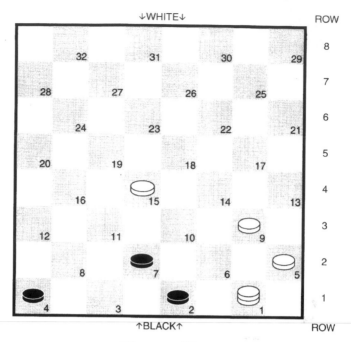

Diagram 53

Black's behind in both checker power and development. It's his turn to go. He spots and makes a game-clinching sacrifice move from 7 to 10. White has to jump from 15 to 6. Then, after black moves his checker on 4 to 8, it's white's turn. But white can't go anywhere, so black steals a victory from his unsuspecting opponent, who should have easily won this match.

Pinning Can Lead to Winning

Sometimes, in an endgame, you can pin down two of your opponent's checkers and/or kings with one of your pieces so neither of them can move without being jumped, which is a very efficacious use of your forces. This tactic can put your other pieces at a numerical advantage in comparison to those that the opponent is still free to move without incurring a capture. This pinning strategy can win an endgame that was being contested with equal manpower and might otherwise have resulted in a draw. An example of this is depicted in Diagram 54. Diagram 55 illustrates three additional pinning positions that you can use to improve your chances in the endgame.

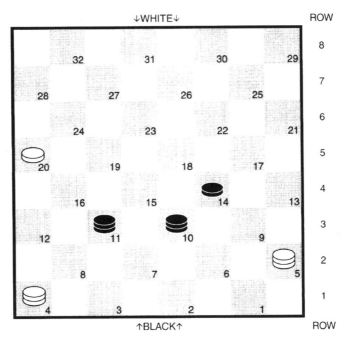

Diagram 54

This pictures the black king on square 11 holding the white checker on square 20 and the white king on 4 at bay. This one-pinning-two technique allows black to move his checker on 14 up the board, unmolested, to get a third king, while white's king on 5 can only shuttle back and forth, helplessly, in the double corner area. As soon as black crowns his third king, he'll bring him right back to smoke white out of the double corner and win!

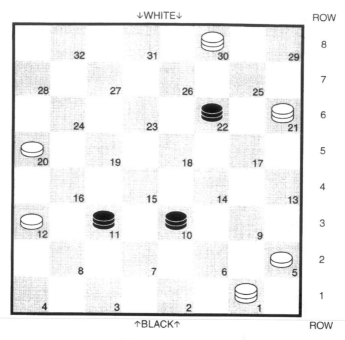

Diagram 55

Diagram 55 has three black kings pinning down six white pieces (three checkers and three kings). While it would be extremely unlikely for all three of these situations to take place in the same game at the same time, they are all common examples of the kinds of pins that thoughtful players look for and take advantage of on offense and defense.

What Is "the Move," Who Has It, and How Can You Use It?
Knowing who has "the Move" can be critically important to winning strategy in the endgame. Having "the Move" must not be confused, as it easily can be, with whose turn it is to go (move). The player who has "the Move" (also called "the Effective Move") is the one who will go last in a game where there are a small and equal number of black and white pieces that, by virtue of their positions on the board, can be forced by the player with "the Move" into an inescapable confrontation. At the confrontation point, the player who does not have "the Move" has to go and must, in doing so, sacrifice his piece for the opponent to jump. It's easy to determine who has "the Move" by counting all the pieces (black and white, checkers and kings) that are on one of the squares in the four vertical columns that start with the four numbered squares in each player's back row and run all the way to the other end of the board. The four columns that start on and go up from squares 1, 2, 3, and 4 in

black's back row are referred to as black's system. The other four columns starting in white's back row on squares 29, 30, 31, and 32 and running to the other end of the board make up white's system. The player whose turn it is to go can determine who has "the Move" by counting all the pieces in his system. If it is an odd number, he has "the Move." If the count is an even number, then the other player has it. There is no use in making this calculation until it is your turn to go, since positions will change by that time and you would have to recalculate accordingly. You can use the column depictions and designations in Diagram 56 to mathematically determine who has "the Move." Knowing who has "the Move" can often be utilized to win or to tie instead of losing. The following diagrams will help you to understand how this concept works. Diagram 57 shows how whichever player whose turn it is to go can win if he has "the Move" in the right circumstances.

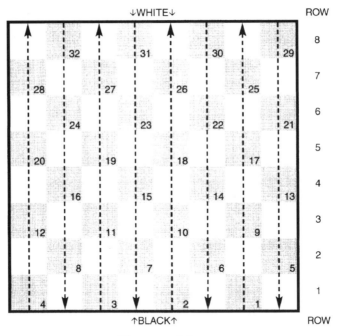

Diagram 56

Black's system consists of the 16 numbered squares in the four columns that start on squares 1, 2, 3, and 4 in row 1 and run up the board to row 8. White's system is made up of the other 16 numbered squares in the four columns that start on squares 29, 30, 31, and 32 in row 8 and run down the board to row 1. Dashed lines with arrows are used in the diagram to clarify the black and white systems.

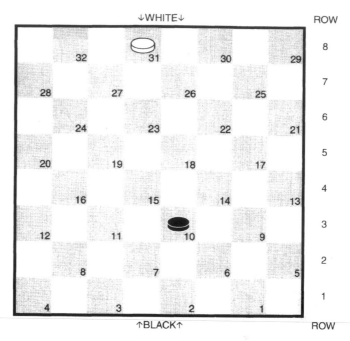

Diagram 57

It's white's turn to go in what might look like an inevitable tie. But it's not. White sees that he has "the Move" with an odd count of 1 when he tallies up the number of pieces in his system (his checker on square 31). He also figures out that he can force a middle-of-the-board confrontation with black by going from 31 to 26. If black replies with 10 to 14, white's next move will be from 26 to 22. Should black play from 10 to 15, white will respond with 26 to 23. In either sequence white will win. If he hadn't calculated "the Move," he might have gone from 31 to 27, which would have allowed black to avoid the losing conflict and draw with 10 to 14. Try it and see.

In some unfavorable situations, where it looks like you're destined to lose because you don't have "the Move" when it's your turn to go, you may be able to turn the tables, get "the Move" back, and win the game, or at least tie it, by initiating a one-for-one exchange. This surprisingly simple but dramatically effective technique of switching "the Move" is diagrammed and discussed in Diagrams 58 and 59.

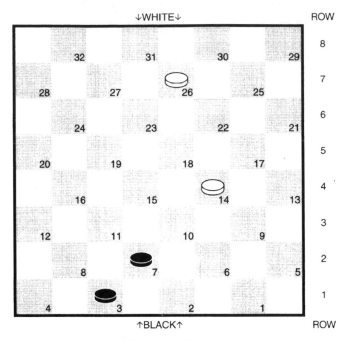

Diagram 58

Although it's black's turn, he doesn't have "the Move" because there is an even-number count of 2 in his system (his checker on square 3 and white's on 26). Black gets "the Move" back to his great advantage with a 7-to-10 exchange that forces white to jump from 14 to 7 and black to jump back from 3 to 10. Now it's white's turn. He has a count of 0 (an even number) in his system so he has lost "the Move," and the game, regardless of which way he goes. If he plays 26 to 22, black will reply with 10 to 14. If he goes from 26 to 23, black will confront him with 10 to 15. In either case white will have to give up his last checker or resign.

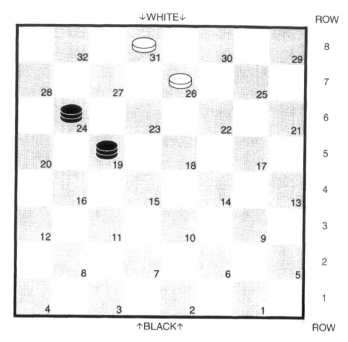

32	31	30	29
28	27	26	25
24	23	22	21
20	19	18	17
16	15	14	13
12	11	10	9
8	7	6	5
4	3	2	1

↑BLACK↑

Diagram 59

White has to go first in what appears to be a losing cause with black's two kings poised to pounce on his unprotected checkers. White doesn't have "the Move," since he has an even count of 2 in his system (his checker on square 31 and black's king on 24). But white refuses to quit. He regains "the Move" with an exchanging play from 26 to 23. Black's king on 19 has to jump to 26 and white jumps right back from 31 to 22. Now it's black's turn again, but all he can do from this position is to chase the white escape artist into the 1/5 double corner, where white will get a king and a well-deserved tie! Another example of persistence paying off.

If a confrontation between the opposing forces can be avoided by the player who does not have "the Move," then having it is of no real value and the game has great potential for resulting in a draw. This is illustrated in Diagram 60.

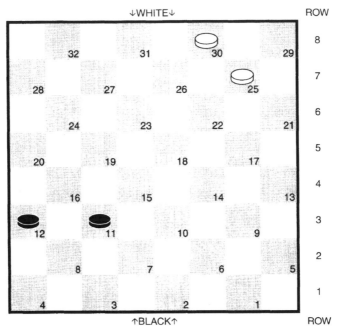

Diagram 60

Black has an odd-number count of 3 when he adds up the pieces in his system, and because it's his turn to go, he has "the Move." But it is of no consequence, because black cannot do anything to force the white checkers into a confrontation. If black goes from 11 to 15, white will reply with 25 to 21 or 22 and continue moving both of his checkers up the left-hand side of the board (from white's perspective) to his king row for a draw.

There is an exception to this complicated rule, which has already been made difficult to explain and understand because of the confusing terminology. It takes place when a player has one of his checkers immobilized in the doghole (square 28 for black and square 5 for white, with an opponent's piece on square 32 or square 1, respectively), which happens quite frequently. In such cases, "the Move" rule is reversed. If it is a player's turn to go and he has an even number of pieces in his system, with an opponent's checker stuck in the doghole, then the player whose turn it is to go has "the Move." Should he tally up an odd number, the opponent would have "the

Move." An example of this exception is illustrated in diagram 61. It shows how this special circumstance gives "the Move" to the player with an even-number count in his system and how he can use it effectively. Should both players each have one of their checkers stuck in the dogholes at the same time, each can determine who has "the Move" when it is his turn to go by the regular odd-number count.

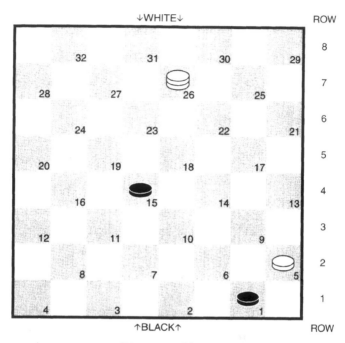

Diagram 61

It's black's turn. White has an immobilized checker on square 5 in the doghole. The inability to make a play with a piece reverses the counting process to determine who has "the Move" from odd to even. In this case, black counts an even number of 2 pieces in his system (his checker on square 1 and the white king on 26). So black has "the Move" and uses it for a win by going from 15 to 18. White's king has to go back from 26 to 30 or 31. Then, black's checker on 18 traps the white monarch by going to 22 or 23, respectively.

Endgame Practice

Some beautiful opportunities to combine position and timing can be uncovered by the imaginative player who is constantly searching for different paths to glory. The chances that crop up are usually very fleeting in nature. They must be spotted immediately and exploited right away, or the position will change and the opportunity will be lost. Diagrams 62 to 66 present real endgame challenges that will test and hone your creativity. Carpe diem!

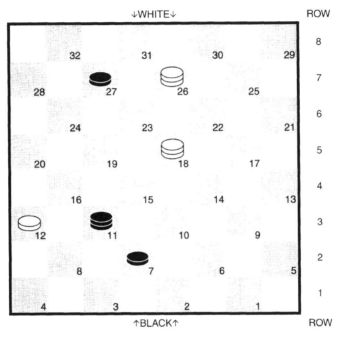

Diagram 62

White's a king ahead in the closing moments of this otherwise seemingly even match with black to move. Black makes sure the moments go by quickly with a super combination play that spells instant doom for white. What's the play?

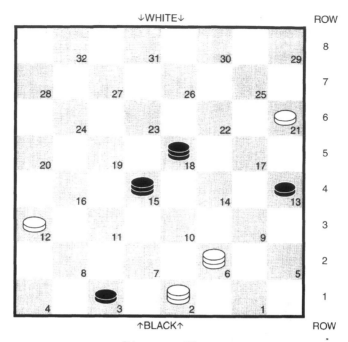

Diagram 63

This looks very much like an endgame standoff. Black goes first and thinks otherwise. He finds a slick way to win that makes it seem easy once it's done. What was black's plan and how did he execute it?

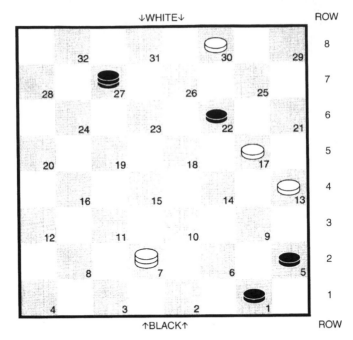

Diagram 64

At first glance, it could be just another evenly matched endgame headed for a tie. It's black's move and he engineers a jumping sequence that earns him a delicious victory. Can you leap to the same conclusion?

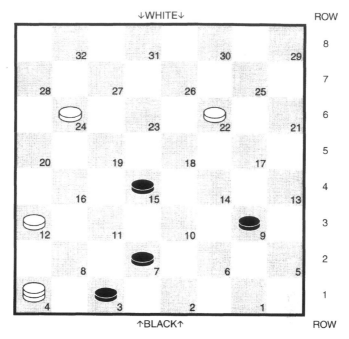

Diagram 65

Black is to move in an endgame where his opponent already has a king that can cause a lot of trouble as soon as it's out of the single corner. Black takes immediate advantage of the initiative with three stunning plays that win the game. White is defenseless against black's dazzling tactics. What are they?

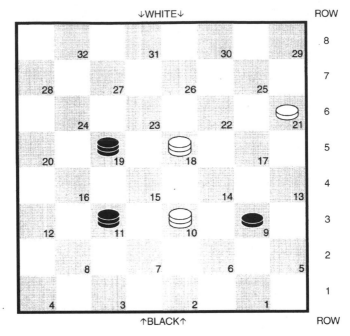

Diagram 66

It's white's turn to move in this endgame where things seem pretty equal in manpower and position. White proves that they aren't equal as he makes three deft moves to put another notch in his victory belt. Can you figure this one out?

Playing to Salvage a Draw

The wisdom of playing with cautious aggression while trying to win in order to be able to fall back to a drawing strategy has been discussed. In the endgame, however, the player at a disadvantage in checker power and/or position should make drawing, instead of winning, his top priority. The outnumbered but resourceful competitor who keeps on thinking ahead in the face of discouraging odds can often turn what looks like a loss into a gratifying tie with careful play and by taking full advantage of his opponent's slightest mistake (and everyone makes mistakes). Two examples of garnering a draw from what appeared to be a lost cause are covered in Diagrams 67 and 68.

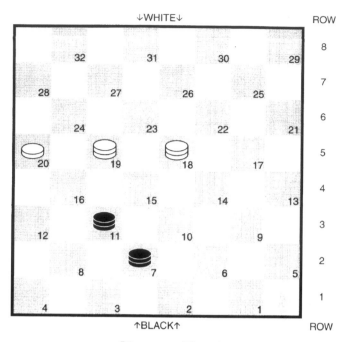

Diagram 67

This is Payne's Draw, a famous, reoccurring endgame that was first recorded by William Payne, a British checker author, in the 19th century. In this exercise, black uses a seesawing defensive strategy with his two kings to prevent the white checker from getting a crown while also parrying white's attempts to lure him into a trap or an even trade that would lead to a two-versus-one loss. The annotated moves that are required to accomplish this are: Black 7 to 10, White 19 to 16, B 10 to 7, W 18 to 23, B 11 to 15, W 23 to 27, B7 to 3, W 16 to 12, B 15 to 11, W 27 to 24, B 3 to 7, W 24 to 19, B 7 to 3. At this point in the struggle, if white moves from 19 to 16, black will go from 11 to 15 and capture white's king on his next move for a tie. Should white move elsewhere, black will continue to utilize the defensively effective seesaw plays to convince white that it's a tie, or black can invoke the 40-move-limit rule to draw.

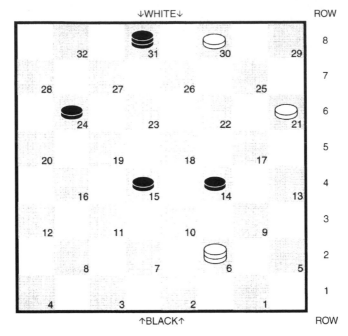

				ROW
32	31	30	29	8
				7
28	27	26	25	
				6
24	23	22	21	
				5
20	19	18	17	
				4
16	15	14	13	
				3
12	11	10	9	
				2
8	7	6	5	
				1
4	3	2	1	

↑BLACK↑   ROW

Diagram 68

White's a checker down in this situation and about to move from 6 to 10 with his king to even the score and the game. But just before he does, he realizes that black will respond with 15 to 18 and after he jumps from 10 to 17, black will go from 18 to 22, forcing him to jump from 17 to 26. That would give black's king on 31 a jump back to 22 where he would pin the white checkers on 21 and 30 for a win. But white does find a fabulous way to draw with 30 to 26. Black's king must jump from 31 to 22. Now white's king moves from 6 to 10 and subjects the black pieces to being double-jumped in two different ways! Black has to succumb to one of them and either one will result in a tied game!

Summary

By this time, as we conclude the discussion of strategy and tactics, you should have a greater appreciation of the intricate thought processes that are continuously involved in the fascinating play of this not-so-simple game. The perplexing problems and exciting opportunities that are created within the simplistic rule system are further elevated by across-the-board play against a competitive opponent. This should stimulate even a casual participant to learn more and become more involved. Playing experience with checkers is (as it is with so many avocations) a great teacher. So to become a better checker player it's important to study, think about, and play the game. In return, it will provide, as it has for so long and so many, an endless adventure of discovery and enjoyment.

Playing the Game

Now that the checker fundamentals have been covered, along with a lot of the strategy and tactics that are involved with this challenging pastime, let's learn some more by playing along with the experts in a championship match from the 1974 Southern Tournament between Marion Tinsley (with black) and Elbert Lowder (another grandmaster, with the white pieces).* Tinsley drew the three-move ballot. The movements, which you might want to set up and follow on your board, went as listed below:

B 11–15, W 21–17, B 9–14 (this ended the three required moves indicated on the ballot card). The game continued with W 25–21, B 15–19, W 24–15, B 10–19, W 23–16, B 12–19, W 17–10, B 6–15, W 30–25, B 5–9, W 22–18, B 15–22, W 25–18, B 7–10, W 18–15. At this juncture the checkers were positioned as shown in Diagram 69.

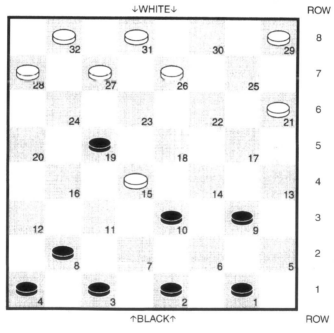

Diagram 69
Tinsley versus Lowder match position after 18 moves

---

*From the annotated game in *Checkers the Tinsley Way* by Dr. Robert L. Shuffett (Hub Publications, 1982).

Post-play analysis shows that Lowder's 18–15 move led to his demise, because it later allowed Tinsley to navigate safely into the king row. If white (Lowder) had, instead, gone 18–14 or 29–25, he might have been able to tie. Tinsley moved 1–6, and the continuation went W 29–25, B 10–14, W 27–23, B 8–12, W 23–16, B 12–19, W 32–27, B 4–8, W 25–22, B 14–18, W 22–17, B 18–22, W 17–13, B 22–25, W 26–22, B 25–30 (for a king), W 22–18, B 30–25, W 21–17, B 25–21, W 17–14, B 19–23, W 14–5, B 23–32 (jumping in for a second king). The locations of the combatants' pieces at this stage are depicted in Diagram 70 and show that Tinsley has essentially won the game.

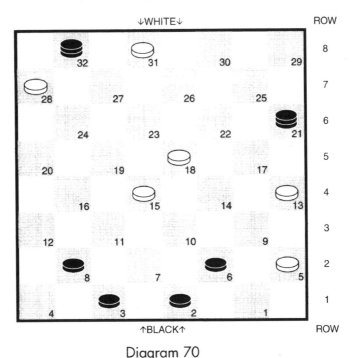

Diagram 70

Tinsley versus Lowder match positions after 43 moves (Lowder resigns)

Lowder resigned, but had he continued, Tinsley would have moved his kings out on a relentless attack to dash any hopes of a draw. Note that Lowder cannot move 5–1 for a king in the Diagram 70 situation, because black would reply with 2–7, forcing the new white king to jump 1–10 and giving black a double jump in return, from 7 to 14 to 23. To the victor go the spoils. Tinsley also won this tournament, as he did so many times.

The Greatest Checker Player Ever: Dr. Marion Tinsley

Dr. Marion Tinsley (1927–1995) is, by all standards, the greatest human checker player of all time. With the advent of ever-increasingly sophisticated computer programs that deal with checkers, he may well remain so indefinitely. He won every major championship and lost only 22 published games to his non-computer opponents over a span of fifty years (1945–1995). He was the only human to defeat the Chinook computer program in a match* after it was fine-tuned. His amazing insight and imaginatively resourceful play earned him the nickname of "The Terrible Tinsley." It was a terrible misnomer for this

mathematics professor turned evangelical minister, who was the epitome of graciousness on or away from the checkered squares that he dominated so well for so long.

---

*The World Man vs. Machine Championship Match, London, August 1992. Tinsley and Donald Lafferty, a U.S. Champion of great renown, have since had drawn matches against Chinook. Lafferty won the U.S. National Championship in Dallas, August 1994, with honor points that broke a dead heat for first place between Chinook, Tinsley, and Lafferty. All their games against Chinook in this tournament were drawn, as were games between each other.

Checker Tournaments

A checker tournament can be an exciting, fun adventure as players match wits in friendly competition against a series of opponents.

Running a tournament is another story. It is a demanding, detail-oriented responsibility that requires foresight, preparation, flexibility, quick thinking, and a sense of humor. These factors increase in importance as the number of entrants grows and as their ages diminish.

Round-robin tournaments are best suited for checkers. They are easy to understand and to follow and to use in conjunction with large groups. They also include a scoring system that takes ties into account, so that two players who have drawn in a match can move on to play their next opponents instead of playing another game to decide on a winner (which could also end in a tie).

This style of tournament schedules every player against all the other players in a group on a rotational basis as shown in the pairing tables on pages 96 and 97. This works fine in relatively small groups given enough time. For instance, 12 players could play 20-minute games with each of their 11 opponents in less than four hours. The scoring is 2 points for a win, 1 point for a draw, and 0 points for a loss. If two or more players are tied with the most points after the 11 games have been played, a playoff would be necessary to determine the winner. With even smaller groups, each contestant can play every opponent twice, which gives everyone an equal opportunity to go first and second. If only one game per round is to be played, a coin flip or some other agreed-upon method of deciding who goes first is used.

Adhering to a specific time schedule for each round of games is necessary to move the tournament along expeditiously. Some people move very fast (usually not a good idea because they aren't thinking ahead), while others agonize over every move. In major ACF tournaments each player is required to make 30 moves in an hour (failure to do so results in a forfeited loss). Some plays, such as a mandatory jump, only take seconds. In more casual events 20 to 30 minutes per game should suffice. If a game has not been decided by the end of the allotted time, the player with the most pieces on the board (checkers and kings are both counted the same in this calculation) is declared the winner and is awarded 2 points. Should both players have the same number of pieces left on the squares when time is up, it's a tie and they each receive 1 point. This tie factor is the reason that ladder tournaments, such as those used in tennis tournaments, are incompatible with checkers, since a drawn match would require all the other contestants to wait idly by while it was played off.

The amount of time available and the number of players involved should determine the format. For instance, if there were four hours available, with 24 entrants, it would be impossible to complete a round-robin event where everyone played a game against each of the other twenty-three competitors, even if all the games were limited to twenty minutes ($23 \times 20 = 7$ hours and 40 minutes). But by dividing this contingent into four groups of six players and following the appropriate round-robin pairing schedule, each player would be matched against the other five people in his group. These five games for each player could be completed in less than two hours ($5 \times 20 = 1$ hour and 40 minutes plus another 15 minutes for scoring, getting to the next match assignment, and setting up to play). Then the four group winners could play a three-game round robin for the championship. Even if the time for these games were extended to 30 minutes, it would take only a little over an hour and a half to establish a champion and would fit well within the four-hour time frame.

Age considerations need to be taken into account in youth-oriented tourneys. It's important to divide the players into age level sections, such as 6–7, 8–9, and 10–11. If time constraints and/or the number of players dictates, ages 6–8 and 9–11 should suffice. In a classroom or same-grade school tournament this would not be an issue.

Checker rules are simple and straightforward. They can be altered as long as everyone is aware of the particular set that is being used.

The rules being used should be explained before the start, and there should be a question-and-answer discussion. They should be prominently posted during and after play. If a listing of the rules can be copied on the back of each player's scoring sheet, it would be a helpful guide. The American Checker Federation rules in this book provide a good starting point for developing rules that would accommodate a specific situation.

The tournament director (and every tournament should have one) does not need to be a checker expert, but he should know the rules that have been agreed upon and have a copy of them to refer to in case of disputes. All the necessary paperwork (scoring sheets and pairing tables) is contained in this section and can be reproduced in appropriate quantities. Tables, chairs, pencils, an easily visible clock, and enough checker boards and checkers for the number of players (two players per board) are the only other materials required.

Trophies or prizes for the champion and finalist are a motivational plus for the players. They need not be expensive and they provide another incentive to play well, while giving the winners a memorable keepsake. They should be announced and shown at the introductory portion of the event and prominently displayed throughout the session. If there is more than one division, there should be equal prizes available for the winners in each section.

Tournament Scorecard

Name_____

Division_____

Round	Opponent	Result	Points	Total points
1	____	____	____	____
2	____	____	____	____
3	____	____	____	____
4	____	____	____	____
5	____	____	____	____
6	____	____	____	____
7	____	____	____	____
8	____	____	____	____
9	____	____	____	____

A win counts 2 points, a tie counts 1 point, and a loss counts 0 points.

If time has run out before the game has been decided, count all the pieces that are on the board. Kings and checkers are considered as equal in this tallying process. The player with the most pieces on the board is the winner and gets 2 points. If both players have an equal number of pieces left on the squares, the game is declared a tie and both players are awarded 1 point. The Pairing Tables listed below can be used to fill out the scorecards before the tournament starts so everyone will know whom he is scheduled to play with in each round.

Pairing Tables
Table A for 3 or 4 players

Round	Pairings	
1	1:4	2:3
2	4:3	1:2
3	2:4	3:1

Table B for 5 or 6 players

Round	Pairings		
1	1:6	2:5	3:4
2	6:4	5:3	1:2
3	2:6	3:1	4:5
4	6:5	1:4	2:3
5	3:6	4:2	5:1

Table C for 7 or 8 players

Round	Pairings			
1	1:8	2:7	3:6	4:5
2	8:5	6:4	7:3	2:1
3	2:8	3:1	4:7	5:6
4	8:6	7:5	1:4	2:3
5	3:8	4:2	5:1	6:7
6	8:7	1:6	2:5	3:4
7	4:8	5:3	6:2	7:1

Table D for 9 or 10 players

Round	Pairings				
1	1:10	2:9	3:8	4:7	5:6
2	10:6	7:5	8:4	9:3	1:2
3	2:10	3:1	4:9	5:8	6:7
4	10:7	8:6	9:5	1:4	2:3
5	3:10	4:2	5:1	6:9	7:8
6	10:8	9:7	1:6	2:5	3:4
7	4:10	5:3	6:2	7:1	8:9
8	10:9	1:8	2:7	3:6	4:5
9	5:10	6:4	7:3	8:2	9:1

If there are an uneven number of players in a group (3, 5, 7, or 9), each one of them is given a bye in the round in which he was scheduled to play the missing player. For instance, if there were only 7 players in a grouping, they would use Table C for the pairing schedule. In round 1, player 1 would not have an opponent since there is not an 8th player. Consequently, he would be given a bye in this round and awarded 2 points for an automatic win. In round 2, player 5 would get the bye and two points, just as if he had won, since he was scheduled to play the nonexistent player number 8. In the subsequent five rounds each of the other contestants would receive the bye and score two points in the following order: 2, 6, 3, 7, and 4. This procedure equalizes the scoring situation for all the players in an odd-numbered group. They are each awarded 2 points in the round where they have the bye.

It seems inappropriate to tender good luck wishes to players entering a tournament, since that factor is not involved with checkers. But we do hope you'll play well and always remember the most important rule of the game, which is to enjoy it!

Answers

The following answers to the puzzles that have been presented show some outright victories, while others depict moves and jumps that force the opponent into a serious deficit. In these latter cases, although the advantaged player still needs to make a continuing series of correct moves to earn the win, it is definitely within his grasp. In referring to this section for verification and/or discovery purposes, the use of a numbered board and checkers will make this a fun exercise, while clarifying the solutions.

18. Black starts with a startling 18-to-22 sacrifice that gives white a double jump, 25 to 18 to 9. Then black sacrifices again with 10 to 14, but after white jumps 17 to 10, black gets a triple jump, from 6 to 15 to 24 to 31, and a king! With very careful play, black should win. This chain-reaction pattern of jumps and shots is called a stroke.

19. Black makes an unlikely looking sacrifice from 21 to 25 and white jumps 30 to 21. Next black moves 11 to 16 and white has to jump from 17 to 10, giving the black checker on 6 a double jump to 15 and on to 24. White jumps back 28 to 19. That sets up black for another double jump from 16 to 23 to 30, where he receives a king that will help him win with a few more well-thought-out moves. If white had chosen the 17 to 10 jump first, black would have jumped back from 6 to 15 to 24. Then when white jumps from 28 to 19 or from 30 to 21, black moves from 11 to 16 and takes the double jump to 23 and on to 30 on his next turn.

20. White's king on 27 moves to 24 and black has to go 16 to 20 to avoid being trapped. Then white moves 23 to 18 and black jumps 20 to 27. After that, white sacrifices the checker on 19 by moving it to 16 and black has to jump from 12 to 19, which gives white's king on 15 a fantastic, game-clinching quadruple jump to 24 to 31 to 22 to 29!

21. Black sacrifices 16 to 19 and white jumps from 24 to 15. Then black moves 5 to 9 and white must jump from 13 to 6. Now black has a game-ending double jump from 1 to 10 to 19 that removes all of white's checkers from the board. Black can win with some other moves, but only after a long, drawn-out chase (because white will be able to get at least one king with his man on 24 with which to prolong the battle) if black doesn't utilize the "sudden death," two-for-two exchange strategy described above.

22. Black should move to square 30 to crown a king and bring it out as early as possible to harass the enemy checkers from behind (kings are most effective from that location, and black should win). If black didn't think ahead carefully, he might very well move to square 31 to get his king and threaten white's checker on 27. In that case, he would lose almost immediately when white moved 21 to 17. Black would have to jump the man on 27 and give white a triple-jump victory from 28 to 19 to 10 to 1!

36. Black begins with what looks like a crazy sacrifice by moving 14 to 17 and white double-jumps from 21 to 14 to 7. Next black moves his king on 31 to 27, behind the two white checkers, and white's king on square 5 has to jump to 14. That gives black's king a sextuple leaping extravaganza in either direction for a spectacular win! This contrived position is unlikely to be duplicated in a real game, but similar situations do arise for the resolute player who doesn't "throw in the towel" too soon. If white had jumped 5 to 14 to 7 on his first move, his second move would have been 21 to 14, and the results would have been the same.

38. White goes 19 to 15 and black jumps 10 to 19. Then white moves 18 to 14 and black jumps 9 to 18 to give white a double jump from 22 to 15 to 8. Black jumps back from 4 to 11. Next white sacrifices again from 27 to 24. After black jumps from 20 to 27, white gets a triple jump from 31 to 24 to 15 to 8. He's a man ahead and can get a king as soon as he moves to square 4 from 8. Another example of a stroke play.

39. Black offers white another jumping alternative by moving 14 to 17. It doesn't matter which jump white takes first. If he jumps 20 to 11, black will jump 17 to 26 and white has to jump back from 31 to 22. Then black gets a triple leap into the king row from 8 to 15 to 24 to 31. If white first jumped from 21 to 14, black would move 6 to 10. Then white would have to take the 20-to-11 jump to give black a double jump from 10 to 17 to 26. Next white has to jump back from 31 to 22 and black executes the aforementioned triple vault!

40. White uses the threat to great advantage by going from 17 to 13. Black jumps 16 to 23 and white does likewise from 13 to 6, giving black a jump back from 2 to 9. This opens up the king row and white leaps right in with a triple play from 27 to 18 to 11 to 2, where he gets a king that he can put to good use in securing a relatively easy victory.

41. White moves 19 to 16 and black jumps 12 to 19 (if B 11–20, W 22–17, B 13–22, W 25–4). White jumps back from 23 to 16 and black has to leap from 11 to 20. Then white sacrifices from 22 to 17. Black must jump from 13 to 22 to set up white's checker on 25 for a triple hop all the way to the king row (25 to 18 to 11 to 4). White should have smooth sailing to the winning finish line from here.

42. Black starts with a 15-to-19 sacrifice and white jumps from 23 to 16. Black replies with 12 to 19, so white jumps 24 to 15. Black gives up another checker with 9 to 14, forcing white to jump from 18 to 9. This allows black's man on 11 to double-jump to 18 and then to 25. White's man on 9 will be captured on black's next turn. Note that if white's checker on 21 moved now, black would get another double jump.

45. White sacrifices 22 to 18 and black jumps 15 to 22. Then white sacrifices again from 17 to 14 and black must jump from 10 to 17. Next white moves out of his back row from 31 to 27, letting black's man on 22 jump to 31 for a king. But that is the end of the party for black. Now white moves 5 to 1 for his king. Then, after black's newly crowned king jumps from 31 to 24, white's royal highness takes off on a quintuple hurdling exercise that will allow him to trap black's two remaining checkers in the single corner within five moves after the carnage has been swept from the board. Fantastic foresight on white's part!

46. White starts with a sacrifice from 22 to 18 and black jumps from 15 to 22. White's king jumps that checker from 17 to 26. Now black's only good move is 28 to 32 for another king. Then white gives up the man on 27 by going to 24 and black jumps 19 to 28. Next white's king goes from 26 to 23 and black is stymied! Every move black makes from now on gives white an unanswered capture. So even though black outnumbers white six to five, he loses. This reinforces the importance of position and timing.

In this problem if black had moved from 19 to 24, the white checker on 27 would have jumped him, going from 27 to 20. If black had gone from 19 to 23, either the white checker on 27 or the white king on 26 would make a capturing leap. Any of these scenarios would leave black at a one-man deficit (five black pieces to six for white). Black's checker on 28 would be the only one he could move without being jumped again and he wouldn't be able to move this new king with any real degree of flexibility. White would go on a carefully planned one-for-one swapping spree and get another king that would inevitably destroy the rest of the poorly positioned dark forces.

47. Black springs a surprising series of sacrifices on his startled opponent. First he goes 18 to 22 and white jumps 25 to 18 (white has to jump 25 to 18 because 26 to 17 would give black an immediate double jump into the king row, 13 to 22 to 29, and an early opportunity to wreak havoc on the depleted and poorly positioned white army). Next, 3 to 8 forces white to leap from 12 to 3 for a king. Then black makes an even trade moving from 13 to 17, and after white jumps 21 to 14, black jumps back from 10 to 17. Now white's new king on 3 must jump to 10 and black gets a beautiful triple jump into his king row from 6 to 15 to 24 to 31. The black king will move right out to chase down the remaining white checkers.

48. Black shocks white with 3 to 7 to give him a jump from 12 to 3 and a king. Then black moves 9 to 13 and the new king must jump to 10 or the checker on 15 has to jump to 8. In either event, black gets a double jump into his king row from 13 to 22 to 31. And on his following turn, after white's taken whichever jump he has left, black will have a triple capturing sequence from 6 to 15 to 22 to 29 to earn another crown and a win.

49. An initial black sacrifice sets the stage with 9 to 14. White jumps 18 to 9. Black goes 13 to 17 and white jumps 21 to 14. Now black has two jumps to choose from—10 to 17 or 6 to 13. He picks the latter (6 to 13) because that forces white to leap from 15 to 6. This sends black on a capturing spree from 2 to 9 to 18 to 27. Now he has a four-to-three manpower advantage, and he's about to get a king to wrap up a victory.

62. White thinks black has lost his mind when he moves his only king from 11 to 8! White jumps 12 to 3 for a third crown. He won't have it for long, because black moves from 27 to 31 for a king of his own. After white's new king jumps from 3 to 10, black wipes out the light-colored monarchy in one fell triple-jumping swoop from 31 to 22 to 15 to 6, and the game goes to the black marauder.

63. Black sets white up for a fast fall by moving from 3 to 7. White's king on 2 jumps to 11 and black's king jumps right back from 15 to 8. But that gives the white checker on 12 a jump to 3 and another monarch to replace the one he just lost. But it's to no avail. Black sacrifices from 13 to 17. After white jumps from 21 to 14, black's king on 18 double-jumps to 9 and on to 2. He'll trap white's king in two more moves to win.

64. Black's first play is 5 to 9 and white jumps from 13 to 6. Black jumps back from 1 to 10 and that gives white's king on 7 a jump to 14. White's ahead in checker power by three to two, but not for long. Black goes from 22 to 26 and the white checker on 30 leaps to 23. It's all over! Black's king on 27 double-jumps to 18 and on to 9, trapping white's last checker immediately after his flabbergasted opponent's next move.

65. This particular position and moment present black with his only realistic opportunity to avoid a tie or a loss, and he makes the very most of it by moving from 15 to 19. White jumps from 24 to 15 and black sacrifices again from 7 to 11. White has to jump from 15 to 8. Then black goes from 9 to 14, which seals the lid on white's coffin. White can't move any of his pieces in the single-corner area, so his man on 22 must submit himself to a game-ending capture. A real bonanza for black!

66. First white goes from 21 to 17 and black has to move from 9 to 13 to avoid being captured. Then white sacrifices his king on 10 by moving it to 15. Black's king jumps from 19 to 10. Now white moves his king on 18 to 14, and after black jumps from 13 to 22, white obliterates the two black kings with a double jump from 14 to 7 to 16. From there he'll trap black in a few more moves. A fabulous winning finish!

Note: If black jumped 13 to 22 on his second move, white would jump 15 to 24. Black would have to go to 25 or 26 to avoid capture. Then white would go from 24 to 19. From this position, white's kings can trap both of black's pieces on the perimeter in three more moves. Black has no way out.

The Other Classic Positions and How to Play Them

In the "Strategy and Tactical Considerations" section, First Position, one of the most common but difficult winning endings, was reviewed. Second, Third, Fourth, and Fifth Positions are discussed here because they all crop up repeatedly in so many endgame situations. Knowing the right moves to make to achieve a deserved victory or to salvage a draw, when defeat seems imminent, will serve you well.

Second Position

Second Position doesn't come up as often as First Position, but it occurs enough to warrant a place in any aspiring player's repertoire. The key to winning is the crowning of two more black kings, while bottling up white's two checkers on the sidelines. It's a tortuous route, but well worth a careful trip to victory, instead of succumbing to a much-less-satisfying draw. Diagram 71, in conjunction with the annotated moves, lights the way.

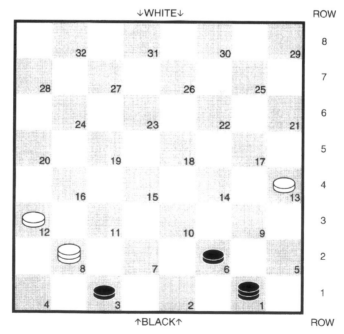

Diagram 71
Second Position

B 1–5, W 8–11, B 5–9, W 11–15, B 9–14, W 15–11, B 14–18, W 11–16, B 18–15, W 16–20, B 15–11, W 20–24, B 3–7, W 24–19, B 7–10, W 19–23, B 10–15, W 23–27, B 15–19, W 27–32, B 19–24, W 32–28, B 24–27, W 28–32, B 27–31 (for a king), W 32–28, B 31–27, W 28–32, B 27–23, W 32–28, B 23–18, W 28–24, B 18–14, W 24–19, B 6–10, W 19–23, B 10–15, W 23–27, B 15–19, W 27–32, B 19–23, W 32–28, B 23–27, W 28–24, B 27–32 (for a king), W 24–28, B 32–27, W 28–32, B 27–24, W 32–28, B 24–19, W 28–32, B 19–15, W 32–28, B 15–10, W 28–24, B 10–6, W 24–19, B 14–10, W 19–24, B 10–15, W 24–28, B 15–19, W 28–32, B 19–24, W 32–28, B 11–16, W 28–19 (a jump), B 16–23 (a jump), W 12–8, B 23–18, W 8–3 (for a king), B 18–14, W 3–8, B 6–1, W 8–12, B 14–9, W 13–6 (a jump), B 1–10 (a jump). From this position black traps white's king on the perimeter in two more moves. This careful, aggressive process took more than 40 moves for both sides. White couldn't use the 40-move limitation to get a draw in this situation, however, because black was improving his chances by crowning his checkers while holding white's at bay. If a player is on the offense and appears to be making progress, the 40-move limit cannot be invoked.

Third Position

Third Position, as illustrated in Diagram 72, is another tedious trail that requires the utmost patience from the player with the upper hand as he strives for a third king to make his day. One miscue could put this contest into a draw. There are several variations that the aggressor must be able to handle depending on the defender's machinations. None of them are harder to deal with or take as long as the version listed below:

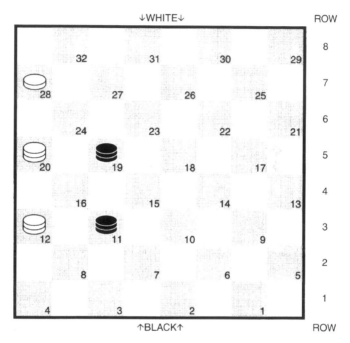

Diagram 72
Third Position

W 20–24, B 11–15, W 24–27, B 15–11, W 27–32, B 11–15, W 12–8, B 15–18, W 32–27, B 19–16, W 27–31, B 16–19, W 8–11, B 18–23, W 11–7, B 19–15, W 28–24, B 23–27, W 24–20, B 27–23, W 7–2, B 23–19, W 2–6, B 15–11, W 6–10*, B 11–8, W 31–26, B 8–11, W 26–22, B 11–8, W 22–18, B 8–11, W 10–6, B 11–7, W 6–9, B 7–11, W 9–13, B 11–7, W 13–17, B 7–11, W 17–21, B 11–7, W 21–25, B 7–11, W 25–30, B 19–24, W 18–23. White wins from this layout. He cannot be denied a third king now that he has split up the two black kings.

*At this point in the hunt, the pieces are located as shown in Diagram 73.

105

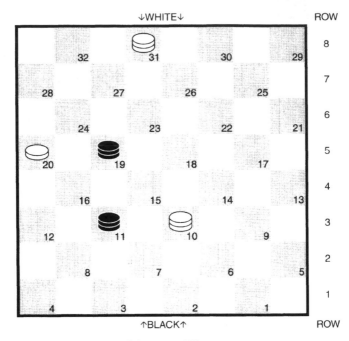

Diagram 73
Third Position—Alternative sequence

If, in Diagram 73, black moved 19 to 23 instead of 11 to 8, white would adjust to this defense by going from 10 to 14 and the play would continue B 23–19, W 14–18, B 19–24, W 18–23, and it would be about over. In a few more moves white will crown the checker that's now on square 20. He's separated the black kings, so he can force one of them into an even exchange for an automatic two-against-one triumph. Each of these games is decided in less than 40 moves by both players from the positions portrayed.

Fourth Position

Fourth Position has a different twist to it. As shown in Diagram 74, it can be won by the player with numerical superiority if it is that player's turn to go. Or, if it is the disadvantaged player's turn to move, he can force a tie.

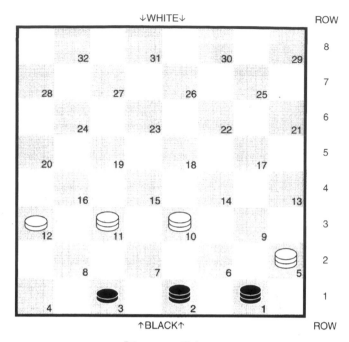

Diagram 74
Fourth Position

In the first case, it's white's turn and he can guarantee a win with the following sequence: W 5–9, B 1–5, W 9–13, B 5–1, W 11–15, B 2–6, W 10–14, B 6–2, W 14–9, B 1–6, W 9–5, B 6–1, W 15–10, B 2–6, W 10–7, B 3–10 (a jump), W 5–9, and there is no way for black to save his king on square 6. If he moves it back to square 2, white will make a sacrifice move from 9 to 6 and get a double jump from 13 to 6 to 15 after black jumps from 2 to 9. If black moves his checker on 10 to 15, white will jump from 9 to 2, splitting up the two remaining black pieces and winning with the three-versus-two strategic process that is shown and discussed in Diagram 51.

Had it been black's turn to move first from this position, he could have forced a tie with these plays: B 2–6, W 10–14, B 6–2, W 14–9, B 1–6, W 9–13, B 6–1, W 11–15, B 2–6, W 5–9, B 6–2, W 15–10, B 2–7, W 9–14, B 7–2, W 14–9, B 2–7 (B 1–5 at this point would allow white to get an even exchange by moving 9–6 so that black would have to jump 2–9 and white would jump back 13–6 for a fairly quick victory). Careful defensive play on black's part from here on will assure him of a seesawing continuation and a well-deserved draw instead of a loss. This illustrates the importance of knowing where you stand and what you need to do to accomplish your objectives from either side in Fourth Position—a not infrequent occurrence.

Fifth Position

Fifth Position, as shown in Diagram 75, is a classic endgame. Neither player has gotten any kings. It's black's turn and, although both players have five checkers, he appears to be in grave danger of losing a man to white and not getting one back in return.

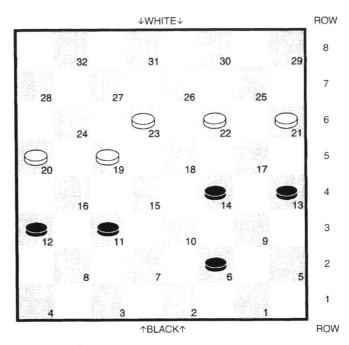

Diagram 75
Fifth Position

If black moves from 6 to 9, white will reply 22 to 18 and capture the black checker on 11 after black goes from 13 to 17 (his only safe play) by moving from 19 to 15. Should black go 6 to 10, white will still move from 22 to 18 to trap the black checker on 14. Either way, black would be a man down and white should prevail in a long but futile (for black) battle. Instead, black uses a sacrificing strategy by moving from 13 to 17 and white jumps from 22 to 13. The game continues as annotated below and results in a gratifying draw for the beleaguered army in black: B 6–10, W 13–9, B 11–15, W 9–6, B 15–24 (a jump), W 23–19, B 24–27, W 6–2 (for a king), B 27–31 (for a king), W 2–6, B 31–27, W 6–15 (a jump), B 27–24, W 20–16, B 14–18, W 15–22 (a jump), B 24–15 (a jump). This sets up the draw. White's checker on square 16 will be jumped and captured on black's next turn to even the score and tie the game for the student who mastered Fifth Position. Try it on your board—you'll like it!

The Longest Stroke Problem and Solution

A stroke in checkers consists of a series of moves and jumps that are initiated and completely orchestrated by the player who is going to win. He makes the first move, which is always a sacrifice or a forcing move, that leads the destined-to-lose opponent into a series of plays (most often jumps) that inexorably result in his downfall.

Working on the solutions to stroke problems is a fascinating pastime that reveals, in an exciting way, the great depth of thought and foresight that is required to capitalize on the kaleidoscopic number of combination plays that are involved in this game. Even more important, these stroke exercises improve the player's ability to spot or sight these kinds of situations as they develop over the board in actual games. By doing so, the alert player can take advantage of them offensively and avoid them from a defensive standpoint.

The longest stroke problem on record was constructed by W. Veal of Southampton, England, and published in *Draughts World* in 1910, with 28 pieces being swept off the board in a dramatic series of plays. It is shown and annotated in Diagram 76, which will be almost impossible to follow without setting it up on a numbered board and carefully making each of the listed moves, jumps, and multiple jumps.

Note: While stroke problemists follow all the standard rules of play, they do not always confine their creations to normally achieved checkerboard positions or to the 12-pieces-per-player limitation, as illustrated by Veal's awesome puzzle and spectacular solution, which starts with 29 pieces located on squares that, in many cases, would be impossible to get to in the regular course of a real game.

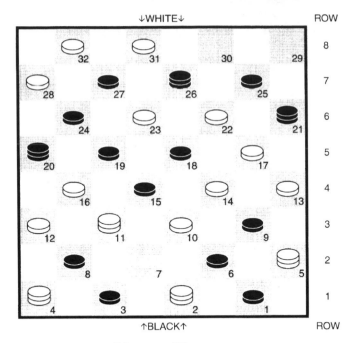

Diagram 76

The longest recorded stroke in checker history—white to move and win

	White	Black		White	Black
1.	10–7	3–10	8.	13–6	1–10
2.	14–7	21–14	9.	11–9	20–4
3.	12–3	26–17	10.	3–8	4–11
4.	4–8	19–26	11.	9–14	10–17
5.	32–23	18–27	12.	2–6	11–9
6.	31–22	17–26	13.	5–32!	
7.	28–10	6–15			

White wins with a quintuple jump!

Rules of Play and Laws for Standard American Checkers

The following rules and laws govern the play and conduct of the participants in officially sanctioned ACF tournaments. They are also very close to the dictates of the British Draughts Federation (BDF). Clarifying comments and suggestions regarding some less stringent interpretations for informal contests are included at the end of each section and encapsulated with brackets.

[Each checker player's usual objective is to win the game by capturing all of the opponent's pieces or blocking them so that the opponent cannot move or jump when it is his turn to go. If neither of these results can be achieved by one player or the other, the game is a tie.]

1. The official checkerboard to be used in national tournaments and official matches shall be green and buff with two-inch squares. The board shall be placed for playing so that the green double corners are on the right-hand side of the players. [Checkers can be played on boards with squares of almost any size as long as there are 32 dark-colored squares alternating with 32 light-colored squares in the famous checkerboard pattern. It is very helpful to have the dark squares sequentially numbered from 1 to 32 as shown throughout this book. Squares 1 and 5 along with 28 and 32 form the two double corners cited above. Squares 4 and 29 are called single corners. Buff is an off-white or very light yellowish color.]

2. The official checkers to be used in national tournaments and official matches shall be turned and round, red and white, and of a diameter not less than one and one-quarter inches nor more than one and one-half inches. The pieces shall be placed on the green squares. [The 12 light and 12 dark checkers can be made up of any two contrasting colors. They should be disk-shaped and sized to fit easily within the dark squares. The 12 dark checkers go on the squares nearest the player who moves first (squares 1–12). The light checkers go on the 12 dark squares nearest the player who goes second (squares 21–32).]

3. At the beginning of the contest the players shall toss for colors. The first move is made by the player having the red (called black in textbooks) checkers. Thereafter, the players shall alternate in leading off with red in each succeeding opening balloted. [Most informal games will not involve the ballot system, but players do continue to alternate in leading off with the darker checkers, from game to game, regardless of who won the previous game or if it was tied.]

4. At the end of five minutes (if the move has not been previously made) time must be called in a distinct manner by the person appointed for that purpose, and if the move is not completed by the

111

end of another minute, the game shall be adjudged as lost through improper delay. When either player is deaf or partially deaf, a card on which the word "time" is printed in large letters shall be placed or laid on the playing table when it is his time to move. [In casual play, there may be no time limit, or opponents may pick whatever one suits their circumstances. The men can move only diagonally forward, one space at a time to an unoccupied adjacent dark square in the row ahead. If there is an opponent's checker or king on an adjacent square in the row ahead with an unoccupied square on the same diagonal line in the following row, that piece (checker or king) must be jumped. Checkers and kings cannot jump over their own pieces.]

5. When there are two or more ways to jump, five minutes shall be allowed for the move. When there is only one way to jump, time shall be called at the end of one minute, and if the move is not completed at the end of another minute the game shall be adjudged as lost through improper delay. [If a player has more than one way to jump, he may select whichever one he wants, regardless of the number and type of pieces that can be captured (he can make what appears to be or is an inferior jumping selection, if that is what he decides to do). The time limits are up to the contestants in less formal settings. There is no advantage to extensively deliberating when there is only one way to jump, since it has to be taken, and delaying gives the opponent more time to think about his subsequent response.]

6. At the beginning of a game each player shall be entitled to arrange his own or his opponent's pieces properly on the squares. After the game has opened (a move has been made), if either player touches or arranges any piece, without giving intimation, he shall be cautioned for the first offense, and shall forfeit the game for any subsequent offense of this kind. If a person whose turn it is to play touches one of his playable pieces, he must either play it or forfeit the game. [Intimation is saying "Adjusting" or "I adjust." A more easygoing interpretation of this rule is to allow a player to touch, move, or even jump with a piece and declare his turn ended only when he removes his hand from the piece that has been repositioned to another square. In other words, a player can still take the move back to its original location and move or jump with another piece instead, as long as he doesn't take his hand off the piece first moved before it is returned to the square that it started from.]

7. If any part of a playable piece is played over an angle of the square on which it is stationed, the play must be completed in that direction. Inadvertently removing, touching, or disturbing from its position a piece that is not playable, while in the act of jumping or making an intended move, does not constitute a move, and the piece or pieces shall be placed back in position and the game continued.

[See comment for rule 6.]

8. The "huff" or "blow" is hereby abolished. All jumps must be completed, and all jumped pieces must be removed from the board. [When the "huff" or "blow" rule was in effect, if a player did not see an available jump and made another move his opponent's options were to:

A. Let the move made remain in force.

B. Remove one of the pieces that could have jumped and make his move.

C. Require a retraction of the move and insist that a jump be taken.

Under the current rules a jump must be taken. If a player makes another move instead of jumping, the opponent has to point it out. Then the move is retracted and a jump made. If a player refuses to jump in this circumstance, he loses the game by forfeit.]

9. When a checker reaches the crownhead of the board by reason of a move or as the completion of a jump, it becomes a king. That completes the move or jump. The checker must then be crowned by the opponent by placing a piece on top of it. If the opponent neglects to do so and makes a play, then any such play shall be put back until the piece that should have been crowned is crowned. Time does not start on the player whose piece should have been crowned until the piece is crowned. [The crownhead is the same as the king row or the last row at the opposite end of the board.]

10. A king once crowned can move in any direction as the limits of the board permit. A king can jump one or more pieces in any diagonal direction as the limits of the board permit. When a piece is not available for crowning, one must be furnished by the referee. [Kings can move and jump in any of the four diagonal directions within the confines of the board. They cannot jump over their own checkers or kings. If a piece is not available for crowning purposes, one of the opponent's captured checkers can be placed underneath the new king or a coin can be put on top of it to designate its new status.]

11. A draw is declared when neither player can force a win. When one side appears stronger than the other, and the player with what appears to be the weaker side requests the referee for a count on moves, then, if the referee so decides, the stronger party is required to complete the win, or show to the satisfaction of the referee at least an "increased" (instead of the old wording "decided") advantage over his opponent within 40 of his own moves, these to be counted from the point at which notice was given by the referee. If he fails to do this, he must relinquish the game as a draw. [A player with the weaker side, as shown in Diagram 67 (Payne's Draw), could offer his opponent a draw. If it is refused, he could ask that the 40-move limitation be set in motion, which, with proper play by the weaker side, would result

113

in a draw being declared after the opponent's 40th move.]

12. After an opening is balloted, neither player shall leave the board without permission of the referee. If permission is granted to a player, his opponent may accompany him, or the referee may designate a person to accompany him. Time shall be deducted accordingly from the player whose turn it is to move. [This means a player could leave only when it was his turn to go. Rule 12 would not be in effect during casual play, which would also not include balloting.]

13. Anything that may tend to annoy or distract the attention of an opponent is strictly forbidden, such as making signs or sounds, pointing or hovering over the board either with the hands or the head, or unnecessarily delaying to move a touched piece. Any principal so acting, after having been warned of the consequences and requested to desist, shall forfeit the game. [Common courtesy is all that is necessary to fulfill the "spirit of the law" regarding this rule.]

14. Players shall be allowed to smoke during the conduct of a game, but care must be exercised not to blow smoke across the board, lest it annoy an opponent. If a player is thus annoyed, he may object to his opponent smoking, in which case neither player shall be allowed to smoke. [This and the rule that follows fall into the common courtesy category. This rule may be obviated in official tournaments, as well, because of the ever-expanding bans on smoking in public places.]

15. Any spectator giving warning either by signs or sound or remark on any of the games, whether playing or pending, shall be ordered from the room during the contest. Play shall be discontinued until such offending party retires. Spectators shall not be allowed to smoke or talk near the playing boards.

The American Checker Federation

The American Checker Federation (ACF), with headquarters in Petal, Mississippi, is the largest checker organization in the world. It schedules and runs sanctioned tournaments, conducts membership drives, provides checker materials (especially oriented toward youth groups), answers questions, establishes and updates the rules for the standard game, and publishes the *ACF Bulletin* on a bimonthly basis. The bulletin contains news, articles, tournament schedules and results, annotated games and puzzles, along with historical notes. Interested parties can become members of the ACF for $25 annual dues or get more information by contacting:

ACF
P.O. Box 365
Petal, MS 39465

Variations of the American Standard Game

Just as its universal popularity has resulted in translations of the name of the game into many different languages around the world, so are there numerous variations in the rules, the number of squares on the board, and the amount of pieces used to play the game. These have been developed to fit the fancy of checkerists in other countries as well as some altered approaches to the way the game is played in the United States.

Many practitioners of the American Standard Game look upon these variations as intriguing challenges, while some others consider them to be confusing distractions. For those of the former persuasion, many of the more common variations are briefly described below. More information on most of those presented here can be found in a library or by a Web search.

Eleven-Man Ballot

The rules of this game are identical to those of the American Standard Game (ASG) except that each player starts with 11 checkers instead of 12 and actual play begins after two balloted moves have been made by both sides. In Eleven-Man Ballot, the player with black selects a card from a deck that lists one checker that is to be removed from a square in each player's two front rows, as well as the first two moves that are to be made for both black and white. After those directions are executed, black starts the game action with the first move of his choice. This method produces well over two thousand original possibilities for interesting new lines of play and by doing so makes the memorization of "book" openings uselessly obsolete.

Eleven-Man Ballot games are an excellent test of the contestants' playing ability across the board. They can no longer rely on previously published patterns of play to determine what moves to make. It may also provide an insurmountable or discouraging challenge for computer programmers and their machines due to the myriad of completely unpredictable combinations that it generates (would the solutions obtained be worth the time invested?).

This exciting version of the game, with its emphasis on skill and creative imagination versus the drudgery of rote learning, can do a great deal to reduce the number of boring draws, introduce untrodden pathways to explore, and rejuvenate this wonderful game with a lot of its youthful aspirants, many of whom are initially intrigued by the play action, but, sooner or later, become turned off by the exhaustively monotonous studying requirements that must be undertaken to reach the expert or master level.

Handicap Checkers

Just as golfers of superior ability give strokes to their less skillful opponents in the interest of creating an even match, checker combatants of differing abilities can turn what would otherwise be a foregone conclusion into a more equal and interesting contest by giving fewer checkers to the stronger player and/or starting the weaker player out with a king or two.

This handicap technique is especially effective when a seasoned adult is playing with a youthful beginner who might otherwise be rather quickly discouraged by an unending series of devastating losses or offended by the transparently purposeful losing tactics employed by a well-meaning stronger player who was "throwing a game" to try to maintain his less-accomplished opponent's interest.

Until the novice wins or draws, his handicap can be incrementally increased. As he prevails, the handicap can be gradually reduced and, hopefully, in time, eliminated.

Italian Checkers

The rules are very similar to the American Standard Game (ASG). The board is turned so that a dark single corner is on each player's right. The player with the light-colored checkers moves first. The 12 white or light checkers are placed on the 12 dark squares nearest to him. Single checkers are not allowed to jump kings! The only other differences are that if a player has more than one way to jump he must:

1. Select the path that will capture the greatest number of the opponent's pieces (checkers and kings both count as one unit).

2. Capture the greatest number of units with a king, if possible.

3. If there is more than one way to capture the greatest number of units with a king, he must take the route that captures the most enemy kings, regardless of where that leaping journey ends.

4. If there is more than one way of accomplishing the requirement in point 3, the path that results in an enemy king's being captured the earliest in the jumping sequence must be taken.

Russian Checkers

As in the ASG, the double corner is on the right, but the light-colored checkers go first. The other changes to the ASG rules are:

1. Single checkers can move only forward, but they can and must jump both forward and backward, just like a king.

2. If a man *jumps* into the king row and has an opportunity to jump right out on the same turn, it must do so. It keeps its new status as a king by being crowned on whatever square it's on when the jumping sequence ends. If a player *moves* into the king row, his turn

116

ends there, even if he has an opportunity to jump back out.

3. Kings can move along as many unoccupied squares as possible on a diagonal line in either direction and capture an opponent's checker or king if there is an empty square in the row behind that piece on the same diagonal. This same king must continue jumping, if possible, on the same diagonal or by making a 90-degree turn and jumping on the other diagonal (the one that is perpendicular to the original line). Diagram 77 illustrates this somewhat bizarre jumping capability.

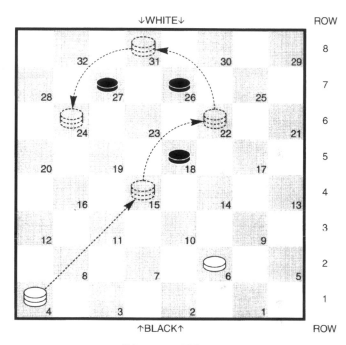

Diagram 77

In one turn of Russian Checkers, the white king on square 4 can move along the unoccupied squares on the diagonal line in front of him (squares 8, 11, and 15) and then jump from 15 to 22 to 31 to 24 to obliterate all of the black checkers for a shocking victory!

4. If the pieces in a game have been reduced to three kings versus one king, the stronger side must capture the lone king within 15 of his own moves or the game is declared a draw. Usually this can be done only if the strong side has control of the diagonal line that connects the two single corners, because of rule 3.

Spanish Checkers

The rules for Spanish Checkers are the same as those used in the ASG except for the following three differences:

1. The double corner is at each player's left-hand side.

2. If there is more than one way to jump, the jumping sequence that captures the greatest number of the opponent's pieces must be taken.

3. Kings can move along any number of unoccupied squares on an open diagonal line up to an opponent's piece (checker or king) and capture it by jumping over it if there is an empty square in the row beyond it on the same diagonal. Diagram 77 at the end of the preceding section on Russian Checkers shows this unusual maneuver that also comes up in several other variations.

Pool Checkers

Pool Checkers is also called Spanish Pool Checkers (not to be confused with Spanish Checkers). This is the second most popular version of checkers in the United States. The rules are almost identical to those of Russian Checkers (as listed above). The only exception is that if a man jumps into the king row and has an opportunity to jump right back out he must take it, but he does not become a king. He can only become a king by jumping into the king row with no jump out or by moving into the king row. In either case his turn ends there with his being crowned.

There are a number of Pool Checker clubs that are affiliated with the American Pool Checker Association (APCA). The listing can be obtained from the American Pool Checkers Association at:

APCA
999 Venetian Way
Gahanna, OH 43230

German Checkers

This game is similar to the ASG in many respects. The rule variations are:

1. The light-colored checkers move first with the dark single corner on each player's left.

2. While men can move only diagonally forward to unoccupied squares, they can and must capture (jump) forward and backward, if possible.

3. If a man jumps into the king row and can jump right back out, it must do so and only becomes a king when it moves into the king row or legally terminates a jumping sequence there.

4. A single checker with more than one way to jump must take the route that will capture the most adverse forces.

118

5. When kings jump, they may land on any unoccupied square on the same diagonal that is being used to capture the opponent's piece (checker or king). The jumping king has to select the square that will enable it to continue jumping in a way that will maximize its capturing activities on this turn if such a square exists (the subsequent jumping can be on the same diagonal or at a 90-degree angle to it). See Diagram 77.

International Checkers

The rules for International Checkers, which is also called Polish Checkers, are the same as those described above for German Checkers, with the very significant exception that the game is played on a board with 100 squares (50 dark squares and 50 light squares alternating by column and row in a 10 × 10 pattern) and each player starts with 20 checkers positioned on the 20 dark squares that are closest to him.

International Checkers enjoys great popularity in the Netherlands which, along with Russia, has produced the best players of this mind-taxing variation over the years.

Canadian Checkers

Also called Montreal Checkers or Quebec Checkers because it originated there, this game is essentially the same as German, International, and Polish Checkers, with two very dramatic differences. The board is further expanded to 144 squares (72 dark and 72 light) and each player starts out with a formidable 30-man army positioned on the dark squares in the first five rows nearest to him.

This more than doubles the squares and pieces involved compared to the ASG. Coupled with the much more flexible and complicated jumping rules for both checkers and kings, this awesome derivation could keep the computer programmers very busy for a long time in a search for the winning solutions to this seemingly unfathomable game.

So too do human players have their hands and minds full to overflowing in trying to achieve any degree of expertise with this melee of possibilities, before succumbing to a serious headache or possible brain freeze.

Giveaway Checkers

This game, which is also referred to as "Loser Wins," is a very different, fun reversal on the ASG. The objective is switched around so that the player who loses all his pieces (checkers and kings) becomes the winner.

Sacrificing as many pieces as possible without having to make a reciprocating jump, and avoiding the conversion of your own men to kings, especially in the early and middle portions of the game, are the keys to losing all your pieces before your opponent can lose all of his, in order to win the contest.

Giveaway games are either won or lost. There are no ties because when the game is played out to the point where both players have one king apiece, the player who doesn't have "the Move" when it is his turn to go will quickly be able to force his opponent to jump his king and will win by losing his last piece. What a concept!

Fox and Geese

This is a short (for attention span), enjoyable, and very easily learned instructional game for children. It bears little resemblance to checkers, except that it's played on the standard checkerboard with four white checkers (the geese) positioned on the four dark squares in the last row at one end of the board. One black checker (the fox) starts from any one of the four dark squares in the row at the opposite end of the board. Players toss to decide who goes first and alternate the opening move from game to game. They may also take turns being the fox and the geese.

Only the dark squares are used for play. The checkers can move only diagonally, one square per move to an adjacent unoccupied square. The geese are allowed to move only forward, but the fox can move forward or backward, just like a king. There is *no* jumping and capturing involved with this game.

The fox wins if he can reach the opposite end of the board by maneuvering in a way that enables him to slip through or around the line of geese as they make their forward moves. The geese win by preventing the fox from making any such penetration, while herding him into a position on one of the perimeter squares where he can be trapped or blocked in a way that renders him incapable of moving in turn (remember, no jumps are permitted).

There are no ties in this game, because the fox either infiltrates the line of geese or they throttle him on a peripheral square. The games never take more than 25 moves apiece since the geese will either catch the fox within that numerical limit as they move forward, or he will have eluded them. Diagram 78 shows both of the above scenarios on the same board.

120

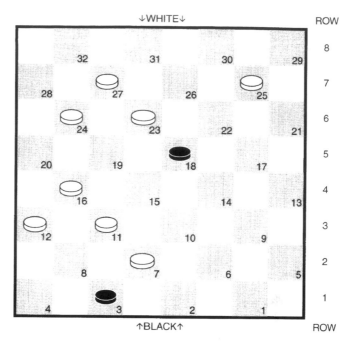

Diagram 78

The bottom half of this board shows the fox about to be trapped in the single corner by the gaggle of geese. He can only move to square 8. Then the goose on square 7 goes to 3 and the fox has to move to 4. Then one of the geese on either square 11 or 12 moves to 8 and it's adios for the black vixen.

On the top half of the board, the black fox on square 18 is going to outfox the flock of geese by moving to 22. Since the geese cannot move back or jump, there is no way for them to stop the fox from going to square 26 on his next turn to elude their clutches and win the game.

Imagination Checkers

As the reader can readily see from all the foregoing variations, there are numerous ways to alter the game of checkers. Imagination Checkers offers opportunities to experiment with additional versions that are limited only by the developer's creativity. For instance, the game could be adjusted to:

1. Start each player out with four kings in the back row.

2. Line 9 checkers up in a triangular pattern to start the game with the apex in the single corner or use 12 apiece starting from the double corners.

3. Allow a king to take his crown off to make two checkers out of one monarch.

4. Give a king that returns to his own back row a second crown that makes him immune to jumps by ordinary checkers.

5. Designate all pieces as kings at the start of the game.

6. Play on all 64 squares (like chess) with different moving and jumping rules. There is a very complex Turkish game that is played like this.

The above list hardly scratches the surface of the treasure chest of possibilities that anyone can utilize to conjure up his version of a dream game and become the world champion with his progeny, if only temporarily.

Since no one has ever been able to completely master the American Standard Game, the serious student who wants to do well at it is more likely to be better served by concentrating his efforts there, while treating all these others as enjoyable, momentary diversions.

The International Checker Hall of Fame

The International Checker Hall of Fame (ICHF) is located in Petal, Mississippi. It is the official international home for checker associa-

tions from all over the globe. The ICHF is housed in Chateau Walker, which was donated to the worldwide checker community by

Charles Walker, a very successful businessman and master checker enthusiast, who is listed in the *Guinness Book of Records* for the most number of simultaneous games played and won (226 games, with 224 wins, 1 tie, and 1 loss). The Hall of Fame, which is available for touring, contains an extensive array of checker memorabilia as well as two of the largest checkerboards in the world.

Checkers, a compendium of information on the game, is issued annually by the staff of the ICHF in magazine form. This is their only official publication and it is designed to promote interest in the game throughout the world. The ICHF can be contacted at:

Post Office Drawer A

Petal, MS 39465

Index

American Checker Federation 114

Answers 98

Blocks 74
Board positioning 12
Breeches 51

Canadian Checkers 119
Chinook 31
Choosing between jumps 18
Color consideration 13
Compulsory jumping rationale 19
Computers 31
Controlling the center 38

Doghole 52
Double jumps 16
Draws 28, 88

Early game 54
Effective move 77
Eleven-Man Ballot 115
Endgame 68, 84
Equipment 11

Fifth Position 108
First Position 73
First to move 12
Fourth Position 106
Fox and Geese 120
Frequently asked questions 28

German Checkers 118
Giveaway Checkers 119

Hall of Fame 122
Handicap Checkers 116

Imagination Checkers 121
International Checkers 119
International Checker Hall of Fame 122
Italian Checkers 116

Jumping and capturing 15

King row, protecting 41
Kings, crowning 20
Kings, importance of 20
Kings, moving and jumping 22
Kings, quickly using 46

Leaving the king row 43
Lowder, Elbert 91

Middle game 61
"The Move" 77
Multiple jumps 40

Numbering 11

Opening moves 14, 54

Pairing Tables 96
Payne's Draw 88
Perseverance 53
Pinning 76
Polish Checkers 119
Pool Checkers 118

Rules 111
Russian Checkers 116

Schaeffer, Jonathan 10, 31
Second Position 103
Simultaneous sacrificing 54
Single checker movement 14
Spanish Checkers 118

Starting position 11
Strategy 33
Stroke problem, longest 109

Tactics 33
Thinking ahead 37
Third Position 104
Ties 28, 88
Tinsley, Marion 31, 38, 91, 93

Tournament scorecard 96 .
Tournaments 94
Triple jumps 17

Variations 115

Winning, by blocking 25
Winning, by forfeit 26
Winning, by jumping 24

What Is American Mensa?

American Mensa
The High IQ Society
One out of 50 people qualifies
for American Mensa ...
Are YOU the One?

American Mensa, Ltd. is an organization for individuals who have one common trait: a score in the top two percent of the population on a standardized intelligence test. Over five million Americans are eligible for membership ... you may be one of them.

• Looking for intellectual stimulation?
You'll find a good "mental workout" in the *Mensa Bulletin*, our national magazine. Voice your opinion in the newsletter published by your local group. And attend activities and gatherings with fascinating programs and engaging conversation.

• Looking for social interaction?
There's something happening on the Mensa calendar almost daily. These range from lectures to game nights to parties. Each year, there are over 40 regional gatherings and the Annual Gathering, where you can meet people, exchange ideas, and make interesting new friends.

• Looking for others who share your special interest?
Whether your interest might be in computer gaming, Monty Python, or scuba, there's probably a Mensa Special Interest Group (SIG) for you. There are over 150 SIGs, which are started and maintained by members.

So contact us today to receive a free brochure and application.
American Mensa, Ltd.
1229 Corporate Drive West
Arlington, TX 76006
(800) 66-MENSA
AmericanMensa@compuserve.com
http://www.us.mensa.org

If you don't live in the U.S. and would like to get in touch with your national Mensa, contact:

Mensa International
15 The Ivories
6–8 Northampton Street, Islington
London N1 2HY England

About the Author

Robert Pike is an American Checker Federation Massachusetts Champion. After graduating from Brown University, he served as a navy jet carrier pilot and then became a sales and marketing executive in the health care industry. He has two medical device patents to his name.

A few years ago, he was introducing his grandchildren to the nuances of the "granddaddy of boardgames," and their genuine interest started him off on an extensive, but unsuccessful, search for a primer on this not-so-simple game. So he wrote *Winning Checkers for Kids* and, for younger audiences, *Checker Power*. Pike also produced an award-winning video, "Learning to Play Better Checkers," to incorporate visualization into the teaching process.

Pike's colorful checker materials and captivating classroom presentations have been enthusiastically received by students and educators, who find that the "magic of checkers" provides a stimulating, multigenerational, interactive challenge that develops critical thinking, strategizing, problem solving, perseverance, and attention span, while also building important social skills.

His checker puzzles have been featured in *Highlights for Children* publications. Bob and his wife, Ann, live in San Diego.

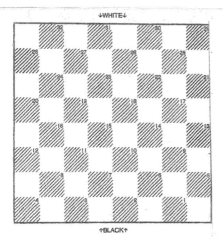

↓WHITE↓

↑BLACK↑

Enlarge to fit your Checkers

Made in the USA
Charleston, SC
27 July 2011